SAVED

SARAH JOY

WESTBOW
PRESS®
A DIVISION OF THOMAS NELSON
& ZONDERVAN

WestBow Press books may be ordered through booksellers or by contacting:

WestBow Press
A Division of Thomas Nelson & Zondervan
1663 Liberty Drive
Bloomington, IN 47403
www.westbowpress.com
844-714-3454

ISBN: 978-1-6642-0364-8 (sc)
ISBN: 978-1-6642-0363-1 (e)

Print information available on the last page.

WestBow Press rev. date: 05/27/2021

To you, because of HIM,
with love

CHAPTER 1

As Jesus was getting into the boat, the man
who had been demon-possessed begged to
go with him. Jesus did not let him, but said,
"Go home to your own people and tell them
how much the Lord has done for you, and
how he has had mercy on you." So the man
went away and began to tell in Decapolis
how much Jesus had done for him. And all
the people were amazed.

Mark 5:18-20 NIV

The Early Seventies
Flint, Michigan

I am a child of divorce—a particularly nasty divorce.
I was three years old when my mother and father parted
ways, too young to understand the situation, but in a
strange way, I'd like to think that what happened between
my parents helped me become the woman I am today.

— 1 —

After the divorce, my parents barely spoke to one another. My mom recovered first, within a year, remarrying an old high school friend and, two years later, giving my younger brother John and I a half-sister, Anna. For the next ten years John and I visited our biological father every other weekend until my mother and stepfather, against his fervent wishes, decided to move us to the other side of the country.

I was fifteen years old when we moved, in the middle of my sophomore year of high school. We lived in Flint, Michigan—the town later made famous (or infamous) by filmmaker Michael Moore.

I loved living in Flint. I was happy and well-adjusted, and enjoyed hanging out with my family and friends. The only thing I didn't like was the cold—and neither did my mother. The previous winter she had slipped on some ice and hurt her back. My mother declared that she was *done* with winter, and that she intended to move our family to a more "civilized" climate.

After much discussion, she and my stepfather settled on Phoenix, Arizona. We were moving from a harsh winter to the Valley of the Sun. Who could say no to that?

Well, my biological father, for one.

He didn't want us to leave. He was furious with my mother (and also with me and John for wanting to go), and went so far as to take her to court. He lost.

My father was heartbroken, as were his parents—my grandparents. My father worked nights at the General Motors plant in Flint, so on the weekend's John and I stayed with him, it was our grandparents who watched us.

John and I loved spending time with Grandma and Grandpa. They lived in a charming home on a lake, and we never lacked for things to do. My grandfather was larger than life—he spoke in a thick Polish accent (his parents arrived in the United States from Poland via Ellis Island), wore a bushy grey moustache on his face, and smoked stinky cigars. He owned a gas station and auto repair shop in one of the poorest areas of Flint. As children, Grandpa let John and I fill up the gas tanks, and sell soda and candy to the kids in the neighborhood.

My grandparents were blessed with three children, nine grandchildren and, ultimately, seventeen great-grandchildren, but they had a magical way of making each of us feel as if we were their favorite. Leaving them was difficult, yet it wasn't until the day we said goodbye that I began to get emotional about the move, and wondered if we were making a mistake.

A few days before we left, my friends threw me a surprise going-away party. As I danced, I noticed several of them crying. This rattled me; I had been so excited about my new adventure that I hadn't allowed myself to think about what—or, more importantly, who—I was leaving behind.

I began to cry myself, and once the tears started flowing, they wouldn't stop. What was supposed to be a joyous send-off turned into one of the most depressing nights of my life. I had grown up with these friends. We had sleepovers and birthday parties. We talked on the phone for hours, went to our high school football games, built homecoming floats, and played in the snow at Christmastime. We watched movies, popped popcorn, and made homemade pizza. In the summer, everyone gathered at my house to swim.

Ours was a close-knit neighborhood. On Halloween we went trick-or-treating, and when we returned home the neighbors fed us hot apple cider and doughnuts. Across the street from my house was a huge corn field; my friends and I played tag and hide-and-seek in that field for hours.

It was these things—the pizza and popcorn parties,

the chilly Halloween evenings, the corn field, and the camaraderie—that I realized I would miss the most.

❧

Two of my uncles helped us caravan from Michigan to Arizona with two cars, a motorhome, and a moving truck. We lumbered down from the mountains of Flagstaff, Arizona at night—in the distance, the lights of Phoenix looked like sparkling diamonds stretched out for miles before us. I grew up in a rural area, so I'd never seen anything like that before. In Phoenix, we pulled into a brightly lit Super Pumper gas station that made me feel nostalgic for my grandfather's gas station in Flint. John, Anna, and I watched as one sports car after another pulled in, country music blaring from their speakers.

We spent our first week in a hotel while my parents—who were both real estate agents and picky when it came to houses—searched for the perfect house, in the perfect location. They finally decided on a neighborhood that surrounded a brand-new high school; my parents felt it would be easier for John and I to fit in if everyone at our school was relatively new.

At my old school, I had been popular, even voted the homecoming princess. Here I felt invisible and, being an apprehensive fifteen-year-old, I was careful who I befriended. I wasn't an athlete and I didn't play an instrument. There weren't any clubs I was eager to join, so that made it even harder to find "my people".

The kids at my new school seemed to move faster than my friends back home. Their parties were wilder, replete with sex, drugs, and alcohol, and I found myself lonely for the first time in my life. I missed my old friends terribly, and in those archaic days before cellphone's, and social media, it was hard to keep in touch with them. Each day after the school bus dropped me off, I would sprint to the mailbox, praying for a letter from home. Those letters from Flint were my lifeline. Reading them, I would daydream about my life in Michigan and wonder why I ever wanted to leave.

∽⋙∾

When James, a cute classmate, asked me to go to a party, I assumed he meant a birthday party. He didn't. When he asked me whether I preferred a joint or a bong, I was speechless—I knew what a joint was, but also knew it wouldn't be particularly cool to ask, "What's a bong?" I declined his invitation.

My life in Arizona changed the day I met Jack in my accounting class senior year. When I transferred into the class mid-semester, Mr. Jones, our teacher, sat me next to Jack and jokingly said, "This is Sarah, your new girlfriend."

Unlike me, Jack was an athlete. He was teammates in three sports with my brother John, and close friends as well. Jack and John were each voted "Super Jock" of their respective class.

Despite my lack of athletic prowess, Jack and I had a lot in common and, to no one's surprise, we were dating within a couple of months. We lived in the same neighborhood, a typical Arizona subdivision with ranch-style homes. Our house was by far the most unique house on our block. When my parents bought it, it was only partially built; it looked as if the owner had been working on it for years. It was an odd house on a large desert lot. It was made of adobe brick, and resembled an old hacienda.

The main house surrounded a square-shaped courtyard

with sliding glass doors on two sides. On the third wall was a built-in adobe brick barbecue with a wood-burning fireplace next to it. On the fourth wall was a detached bedroom with a window that looked into the courtyard. There was also a small guest house in the back.

The courtyard was my favorite part of the house. It was our family's gathering place, and we liked decorating it together. Anna made mason jar hummingbird feeders and hung them from the ficus trees. We happily watched the hummingbirds flutter by as we drank our morning coffee.

In the middle of the courtyard was a tall, beautiful, Mexican stone fountain surrounded by pots of fragrant jasmine. The outdoor dining room table was six feet long, made of wrought iron and sported a glass tabletop. Brightly colored pillows decorated the chairs that surrounded the table. My mother had placed a dozen candles at the center of the table, and positioned two chaise lounges so we could view the stars at night. I loved lying in that courtyard, listening to the fountain and feeling the warmth of the fire.

The courtyard engaged my family's senses, while at the same time giving us the peaceful feeling of having our own sanctuary. This was true desert living, and my family forged many happy memories there.

I was the oldest of the three kids, so I was granted the privilege of living in the detached bedroom. I even had my own gated entrance. My bedroom had a small sitting room, with a door leading to the main bedroom. I had a walk-in closet and private bathroom, complete with an old-fashioned, free-standing, white porcelain bathtub. In the center of my bedroom was a king-sized waterbed covered with a flowered comforter and pillows. I did my homework in an oversized Laura Ashley chair.

My bedroom had a large window that overlooked an

untouched desert of wild flowers, saguaro, and prickly pear cacti. Occasionally I'd see a jackrabbit or a family of quail, and every so often a coyote would howl. Looking out at that desert, I was constantly on the lookout for rattlesnakes, of which I was deathly afraid.

When I began attending college, I worked at a grocery store ten minutes from my house. I was the closing cashier, and usually got home after midnight. Because my bedroom was detached and a short distance from the main house, I could play music or watch television without anyone hearing me.

It was the perfect setup for a working student who couldn't afford to live on her own... until the night I *needed* someone to hear me.

❧❧

I first became aware of the spiritual realm shortly after I began college.

Fast asleep in my bed, I was awakened one night from a deep sleep—not by a breeze, but by a strong, cold wind blowing into my bedroom. Groggy and disoriented, I realized that my waterbed was trembling.

My first thought was that we were having an earthquake. Terrified, I tried to climb out of bed, but something pressed on my chest and pushed me back down. My second thought was that a stray dog had gotten into my bedroom by way of an open gate.

I swung my arms, trying to push whatever it was away... but there was nothing there!

I instantly went into shock.

I felt a hand—or what felt like a hand—grab the inside of my thigh.

Terrified that I was going to be raped, I began to pray. I wasn't religious and didn't attend a church, but I did pray most nights before going to bed. This was a habit instilled in me from the time I was a little girl.

Most of my prayers were prayers of thanks—but on this night, my prayers were brought on from sheer horror.

When I prayed, God's peace immediately calmed me down. Everything stopped—the wind, the bed, and whatever was pressing on me. I continued to pray until I fell asleep. I awoke in the morning, astonished that I had been able to fall back asleep after experiencing something so terrifying.

In the main house, my stepfather was drinking coffee at the kitchen table. When I told him what I had experienced, I expected him to tell me that I must have dreamed it.

But that is *not* what he said.

Instead, he looked startled, and told me he had been awakened twice by a knock on the door that connected the main house to the guest house, where my grandparents stayed during the winters. He assumed it was just his parents knocking on the door. My stepfather answered the door both times, but no one was there. He peeked in on his parents, who were both fast asleep, and then went back to bed.

When my mother woke up, we shared my story with her. Her face went pale, and she said she had heard knocking at the front door in the middle of the night, and assumed I had misplaced my key. She looked out the peephole and saw nothing, so she went back to sleep.

My brother John came into the kitchen and joined the conversation. He said he had heard noises in his closet, but was too scared to investigate.

The four of us sat quietly at the kitchen table, bewildered by what had taken place in our home just hours earlier.

That night, Jack and his friend Chad picked me up to go to a football game. I told them what had happened to me the night before. After listening to their ghost stories and advice, I decided to put a cross and a Bible in my bedroom.

Still, it was months before I dared to sleep in there again.

Years later, after my parents sold that house, they told me that the first wife of the man who sold them the house had committed suicide while living there. The man remarried a few years after that, before my parents bought the home.

I didn't know the Bible then, so I thought that we were being haunted by his first wife's ghost. I know better now… we were under spiritual attack. We were an unbelieving, dysfunctional, undisciplined, blended family. On top of that, there was some "bad blood" where the sale of the house was concerned—the owner had apparently had an attack of seller's remorse on the day of closing.

Looking back, only God knows whether my parents should have bought that house or not.

CHAPTER 2

Jack and I were both twenty-one years old when we got engaged.

Everyone around us was getting married, so it seemed like the natural next step in our lives. The night Jack asked me to marry him, he introduced me to a new song he wanted to be sung at our wedding—*Leather and Lace* by Stevie Nicks and Don Henley.

When he played it, I was delighted. It was the perfect song for us.

Jack and I were engaged for a year, and got married the week before Christmas. Our wedding was a comedy of errors from the beginning—it reflected the fact that Jack and I were young and immature, and that I had done an inadequate job of planning it. For starters, I left Jack's wedding ring at home and had to rush back to get it; this took up the time I had set aside for my manicure. My mother painted my nails at the last minute, so I'm sure I smelled like nail polish walking down the aisle.

To top it off, our wedding was so boring that we couldn't wait to leave our own reception and begin our honeymoon in Snowbird, Utah.

Unfortunately, that didn't turn out the way I had imagined it either. I was an avid skier, and stupidly decided to introduce my new husband, Super Jock, to the sport. Jack fell in love with it. He woke me up bright and early every morning to hit the freezing slopes, insisting that we ski until the lifts stopped running.

Cold and exhausted, I quickly regretted picking Snowbird as the location for our honeymoon. In fact, I began second-guessing *everything* I had committed to in the last week.

One evening, Jack and I bundled up and walked from our hotel to a nearby steakhouse. The restaurant was loud and busy; there was a band playing and a handful of people dancing. We had settled into a booth next to the dance floor when the guitarist asked if there were any newlyweds in the crowd.

Laughing, Jack and I raised our hands. The band asked if we would come out and start the next dance off to a new song they had just learned. Shyly, we agreed.

When the band started singing, Jack and I stood frozen on the dance floor. We stared at each other.

The band stopped playing.

"What's wrong?" the guitarist asked.

"That was our wedding song," I told him.

Both Jack and I thought that the other one had requested *Leather and Lace*, but we hadn't.

When the other patrons realized what had happened, everyone started clapping and cheering.

With tears in my eyes, Jack and I began to dance. We knew that something incredible had taken place.

I believe that God wanted us to know that He was with us.

We didn't have dancing at our wedding, and it wasn't

until decades later that I understood that our Heavenly Father wanted to make sure—right there in that smoky steakhouse—that Jack and I had a proper first dance as husband and wife.

God was blessing the marriage we had just entered into, but Jack and I were too young and naïve at the time to realize it.

CHAPTER 3

T he spiritual realm is a funny thing.

In one way or another, I think we're all aware of it—even if we don't know what to make of it.

Are we living in *their* world, or are they existing in ours? And who are *they*, exactly?

According to the Bible, there's a spiritual war being fought between Jesus and His angels against Satan and his demons. Satan was once a beautiful angel who desired God's position, and who desired to be worshipped. He was therefore cast out of heaven and became the temporary ruler of this world. Satan is a liar and a deceiver. He is also a ruthless tempter who specifically targets those who believe in Jesus Christ. He knows that he already has control over those who don't believe.

Looking back on my forty years of life with Jack, I can see in very obvious ways how Satan tried to tempt us away from each other. We were both young and attractive; I had female friends tell me that Jack was beautiful. One woman went so far as to warn her daughters never to date anyone as handsome as Jack. It was shocking to hear someone refer to my husband in that way.

Because we were so young when we got together, I was oblivious of what men thought of me. Jack was the only man who had ever told me I was beautiful and, frankly, his was the only opinion I cared about.

Until I met Allen. Jack and I met Allen while we were working in real estate.

Allen was the only man who had dared to flirt with me as a married woman. After a few months of his suggestive comments, my head was reeling. On more than one occasion, I walked away from our conversation thinking, "Did he just say what I think he said?"

Although I knew never to cross any boundary that would jeopardize my relationship with Jack, I secretly loved the attention. What girl wouldn't?

I didn't flirt back with Allen, but he knew I liked it. In fact, I more than liked it, since Jack rarely flirted with me. That just wasn't Jack's personality.

I had to work hard not to let Allen know he was getting to me, but he was. Fortunately, I was able to keep my boundaries, weak as they were.

A year or so after Allen came into our lives, Jack and I became unexpectedly pregnant. Soon afterwards, Allen and his new girlfriend moved away.

Sadly, I miscarried not long after that, but for those few weeks Jack and I realized how ready we were to start a family. As soon as the doctor gave us the go-ahead, we decided to try and get pregnant again.

The situation with Allen reminded me of a cartoon I saw of a married couple holding hands; the husband and wife were having separate conversations with members of the opposite sex, and each of them was oblivious to the other's conversation. However, the demon in the middle of the husband and wife was *not* oblivious of their conversations.

He was working hard to break up their marriage—as evidenced by the looks of lust on the faces of the husband and the other woman.

Satan hates marriage. God hates divorce.

Fortunately, in my case, even though I was stumbling, God was winning.

❧

Several years later...

Jack and I went on to live blessed lives, and had a strong and happy marriage. We had three healthy, amazing children—Ryan, Addy, and Wyatt. Jack had a successful career in sales, while I lived the blessed-yet-hectic life of a stay-at-home mom. We loved our extended family and friends, and as far as I could tell, our little family was completely satisfied with its life.

One day, an old friend from work called to say that she had run into Allen—yes, *that* Allen—in Hawaii. In fact, she said that several of our old work friends were happily living on the island of Hawaii, otherwise known as the Big Island. When she shared what their monthly incomes were, neither Jack nor I could believe it.

We knew we had to check it out—if Allen was living there, there had to be something to it. Naturally, I reflected on what had happened between us, but I assumed that by now we were both mature enough to handle it.

Jack and I agreed to take a trip to Hawaii to see what all the hoopla was about. We gathered up our airline miles and took the kids there for their Winter break.

It didn't take long for all of us to fall in love with the island. My kids took to the ocean in ways I never would have anticipated.

One afternoon I was sitting on the beach watching Jack, Ryan, and Addy learning to surf. Two-year-old Wyatt was playing in the sand next to me. I realized that as happy as my family generally was, I had *never* seen them like this before. We were all blissfully content.

To our great surprise, Allen joined us on his lunch break. We hadn't had a real conversation in years. Since we'd last spoken, Allen had gotten married, had a son, and gotten divorced. The divorce was traumatic, so he moved to the Big Island to get a fresh start on life. He was raising his nine-year-old son, Sam, by himself.

Knowing there are two sides to every story, my heart still broke for Allen as I listened to what he and his son had been through. We made plans to have dinner that night and meet Sam.

The trip to Hawaii was our best family vacation ever. We bonded instantly with Sam. Jack toured the property where he would work if we ever moved to the Big Island— and loved it! The town and beaches were heaven on earth, so going home wasn't easy for any of us, especially me.

In one short week, Hawaii felt more like home to me than where I had lived most of my life.

⚶

On the first day back to school after our trip, while dropping Ryan off at middle school, I noticed all the school buses parked in back. The principal was outside, speaking to a crowd of worried-looking parents.

There had been a bomb threat, and I took that as a sign.

I became determined from that day forward to get my family back to Hawaii.

The month before I turned forty, Jack asked me what

I wanted for my birthday. I told him I wanted to return to Hawaii for the summer. I needed to be sure that moving there was what I really wanted.

Jack fought me on this; he didn't want to move anymore. As much as he had enjoyed our vacation to the Big Island, he loved his life in Arizona, and thought it was the best place to raise our family.

I thought the complete opposite. I found myself watching anything I could find on television about Hawaii just so I could catch a glimpse of the ocean and scenery.

I became *obsessed* with the idea of living in Hawaii.

Jack and I even went to marriage counseling over the situation. He didn't want to go back to the island of Hawaii and I did. The counselor asked, "What do you have to lose by giving it a try for the summer?"

That was that. Jack finally agreed to go, and I was thrilled.

Our summer in Hawaii came and went—it was everything we could have hoped for and more. To my delight, Jack fell in love with the island, and agreed that we should move here. At the end of the summer, Ryan asked if we had bought our return tickets yet—he was the only one who wanted to go back to Arizona.

Jack and I didn't know how to break the news to him. Hawaii had already become home for the rest of us, and when we told Ryan we were staying he initially acted confused. But he quickly grew to love the idea of living and surfing in the tropics year-round.

Before school started, Allen asked if I could watch Sam in the afternoons while he was at work. Our families were together often, so it wasn't a hard decision. Besides, Sam was a sweet, easygoing child who was fun to have around. He and Addy had become friends, and he liked playing with little Wyatt.

Before I knew it, not only was Jack working with Allen, but we were constantly socializing with him and Sam. I watched Sam most days of the week, and Allen called me during the day to see how he was doing.

Over time, I noticed that our conversations were lasting longer and longer.

I had known Allen for almost two decades, which was the problem. He had been a bachelor for most of that time, and I knew first-hand what he was capable of. Allen was handsome, charming, and mischievous, and there were times I had no idea what to think of him.

Although I didn't completely trust Allen, I was unquestionably drawn to him. I *wanted* to believe the best in him, but I never knew whether he was manipulating me, or whether he was sincerely a nice guy.

At some point, I realized the situation with Allen was getting out of control. I started looking forward to my time with him, either in person or on the phone, more than time with my own husband.

I was consumed and ashamed by my feelings for Allen, but had no one to confide in. I had gotten into this mess by insisting that my family move to Hawaii.

What was I thinking? I had knowingly put myself into a tempting situation with a man I had once been attracted to. I thought I could handle it, but I was wrong.

For the first time in my life, I turned to the Bible for answers. I read what it had to say about temptation and adultery.

Before I knew it, I was reading about adulterous women. I was confused because my feelings toward Allen weren't sexual, yet I knew that emotionally, I could still end up like the adulteress women in the Bible. After all, I felt irresistibly drawn to Allen, and wanted nothing more than to spend time with him—with or without Jack.

The Bible talks about a wise woman building her house, while the foolish woman tears her house down with her own hands. I realized I needed to be the wise woman for the sake of my family. I decided to tell Jack about my feelings for Allen, firmly believing it was the only way to stop the runaway train all three of us were on.

I confessed everything to Jack, and he handled it better than I expected because, of course, he *knew*. He noticed I was paying more attention to my appearance, the house and meals especially when Allen and Sam joined us. In every other way our life was amazing, so he didn't know what to do about this.

I didn't think I was sharing anything with Allen that crossed boundaries, but that didn't change the fact that I was constantly thinking about another man, when I should have been thinking about my own.

Despite this uncomfortable situation, both Jack and I cared deeply about Allen and Sam. And we certainly weren't ready to move back to Arizona. We loved our life in Hawaii and wanted to make it work. We just couldn't figure a way out of what was going on between me and Allen without hurting two families in the process.

After much discussion, Jack and I agreed to call our counselor in Arizona. His famous last words—*What do you have to lose by giving it a try for the summer?*—were proving to be more than we could bear.

What did we have to lose by giving Hawaii a try?

Everything, it turned out.

Jack and I had a three-way conversation with our counselor. He listened to what we had to say, and was very matter-of-fact in giving his professional opinion.

"You and Allen are not friends," he told me. "This may be an emotional affair. If you want to save your family, you have to end your relationship with Allen. Now... cold turkey."

Our counselor suggested we could take it slower with Sam. It was also up to Jack whether he wanted to continue working with Allen, but the counselor didn't recommend it.

Jack and I hung up the phone and lay in each other's arms, heartbroken and consumed with our own thoughts.

When Allen called the next day, I told him we needed to talk. Because I had never been sure if he was a good guy or not, I was torn about severing my relationship with him.

I knew it needed to end, but I didn't know how I was going to feel when it was over. Was I going to feel guilty... or relieved? The entire situation was overwhelming.

When Allen got out of his car and into mine, I could tell by his body language that he was not expecting the conversation I was about to deliver. And why would he—we were meeting in a parking lot next to the ocean.

Just the two of us.

At sunset.

Remembering that I was the one who put all of us in this dangerous—or at least tempting—situation, I told Allen in the kindest way possible that we could not be friends anymore.

He looked at me in disbelief, muttering "Why?" over and over.

I was unable to move, barely breathing. Allen was convinced that Jack was making me do this. He told me he thought our marriage was bulletproof, and that he could say whatever he wanted to me.

I told him that no one's marriage was bulletproof. The problem was that what he was saying made sense. Sitting there, my guilt overwhelmed me, and I began to second-guess everything.

"What if I'm the bad guy," I thought, "and he's the good guy?"

After all, I was the one who moved my family to the island where he lived. What if I did that just to be near him? What if it had nothing to do with living in paradise? What if it had nothing to do with making more money, or having a blissfully happy, healthy, and safe family?

Nothing made sense to me anymore, and then, without another word, Allen was gone.

Jack and I continued to watch Sam until Allen found alternative child care. After he did, I bent over backwards whenever I saw Sam to show him how much I cared about and missed him.

We missed both of them, and thankfully God led me to a verse in the Bible that made all the difference:

No temptation has overtaken you except what is common to mankind. And God is faithful; he will not let you be tempted beyond what you can bear. But when you are tempted, he will also provide a way out so that you can endure it.

1 Corinthians 10:13 NIV

After reading this verse, I made the decision to believe God's Word, and to believe that He would get all of us through this awful situation.

It took time, but that is exactly what God did.

Our kids knew that something serious had happened, but neither Jack nor I said a word. If the situation was complicated and confusing to us, how in the world were we ever going to explain it to them?

CHAPTER 4

One month after ending my relationship with Allen, Jack asked for some time off work, and we took our family on a much-needed vacation to Kauai—the Garden Isle. Much of that island is decorated by tropical rainforest and flowers, and while each of the Hawaiian Islands has its own unique character, Kauai is my favorite.

Overall, Kauai is quieter than Oahu or Maui, and less crowded; it was exactly what Jack and I were looking for.

On our first day we took the kids surfing in Hanalei Bay. We bought a cooler at the gas station, then stopped at a grocery store for bottled water and deli sandwiches. While in the checkout line, I was startled to see that the cashier had pink eye. I asked Jack to take the kids outside. Knowing how contagious pink eye is, I bought a tube of hand sanitizer and met my family out front. Everyone but Wyatt put on gel—he was only three years old, and I didn't like the idea of putting chemicals on his precious little hands.

After applying the gel, we loaded up our rented SUV and eagerly headed to the beach. It wasn't until we arrived at Hanalei Bay that I noticed my wedding ring was missing!

My mind immediately flashed back to the grocery store. I had taken my ring off when I applied the hand sanitizer. In a panic, I told Jack what had happened. We quickly unloaded the car, then Jack sped back to the grocery store to look for the ring. He searched the table we had been sitting at and surrounding grounds, with no luck. He checked the lost and found, but no one had turned in my ring. Exasperated, Jack filed a report with the police department; he left his cellphone number, hoping someone would turn the ring in before we left to go home.

When Jack returned to the beach without my ring, I began to cry. He and I had scraped all of our money together and bought a heart-shaped diamond when we got engaged. The first time we went ring shopping, we found the perfect bridal set. After we were married, we had them soldered together. It was all very romantic.

Now my ring was gone. I felt convicted because of Allen and Sam, and believed that I didn't *deserve* to wear that ring anymore.

Jack, being typically male, didn't understand why I was so upset about my missing wedding ring, but I knew there was more going on here than simply losing a ring.

To add insult to injury, the next morning Wyatt woke up with a raging case of pink eye!

When we got home, Jack and I went ring shopping several times, but nothing stood out to me. I wanted *my* ring, and couldn't imagine wearing anything else. We tried several different diamond shapes and metals, but nothing piqued my interest.

Jack was frustrated—not because he had to go shopping, but because I wasn't wearing a wedding ring on my finger, and because I only seemed to want my ring or nothing at all.

Eventually, we both stopped thinking about it, and I became accustomed to walking around with a naked finger.

❧

Several months later, Addy came bounding down the stairs, grinning from ear to ear.

"I have a surprise for you," she said.

"What is it?" I said.

Addy held out her hand. In her palm was my wedding ring!

My jaw dropped.

Why would Jack replicate my wedding ring and then have Addy give it to me?

"What's going on, baby?" I asked.

"I just emptied the beach bag we took to Kauai," Addy said, barely able to contain her excitement, "and your ring fell out!"

I was dumbstruck. I stood there looking at my ring, marveling that we hadn't replaced it after so many months, and thanking God for giving me a second chance.

CHAPTER 5

My family is obsessed with basketball. If we're not playing it, we're watching a game on television. My love for the game is nostalgic—the first time I noticed Jack in high school, he was playing in a basketball game against our archrival. Dribbling the ball down the court, I thought he was the cutest—albeit sweatiest—boy I had ever seen.

As our kids grew up, one of my favorite things to do was watch our son Ryan play high school basketball. He was a natural athlete, and his games were exciting to watch. Ryan didn't play college basketball, but during the summer he played in a men's league on the Big Island. That was a bonus for us—not only did we love having Ryan home, it was thrilling watching him play. We planned our entire summer around Ryan's schedule.

One afternoon we were running late to one of his games. As we backed out of the driveway, we noticed a group of our neighbors huddled around an ambulance that was parked in front of one of the homes on our street.

I rolled down the window and asked one of my neighbors

what had happened. Sadly, she told me that someone had overdosed.

I looked at the house, shocked; I couldn't imagine either of the residents who lived there doing drugs. The house was owned by an elderly woman named LuAnn and her middle-aged son, Tim, who worked at a nearby coffee and pastry shop. He was extremely pleasant to us whenever we came in.

Then I remembered that LuAnn subleased her extra bedroom, so naturally I assumed it was the renter who had overdosed.

The victim wasn't anyone we knew so, because we were already late to Ryan's game, we continued on without waiting to find out their fate. We were indifferent to the situation, and we naively assumed that since we didn't know the person who overdosed, we couldn't do anything to help if we stuck around.

After the basketball game, I ran into one of our part-time neighbors at the grocery store. I didn't know Pam well; she lived in Oregon nine months out of the year. Pam told me that the ambulance had been there for Tim, LuAnn's son. For reasons unknown, he had tried heroin for the first time and it killed him.

My knees buckled.

I couldn't believe it. Tim was such a friendly man. He had always been so kind to all of us.

I felt nauseated. Three hours earlier our sweet neighbor had either been fighting for his life or dead, and we had callously driven away, feeling guilty for leaving, but determined not to be late to Ryan's game.

Overwhelmed and ashamed, I thanked Pam for the news and left the store.

When I got home, I told my family that Tim had died.

My kids couldn't believe it; they had never been exposed to death before.

My thoughts centered on LuAnn. I couldn't imagine what she was going through. Tim was his mother's whole world; she absolutely adored her son.

That evening, I went to check on LuAnn. She was devastated, of course, although she acted calmer than I was expecting. A doctor had given her a tranquilizer and was still sitting with her.

I gave LuAnn my condolences and offered to continue checking up on her. Watching LuAnn in her rocking chair, surrounded by pictures of her son, was one of the saddest moments I had ever witnessed.

❧

Several days later, Pam came by our house to see how I was doing. We sat on my front porch and talked for hours. It was apparent to her—and to me as well—that I was not only sad, but headed toward depression.

It was more than just Tim's death. I had been struggling emotionally for several months before he died. In addition to being premenopausal, I was dreading Ryan heading back for his second year at college. His freshman year had been harder on me than I had anticipated. Although Ryan only attended school a couple of islands away, we didn't see him as often as I thought we would. On top of all that, my brother and sister-in-law in Arizona were having marital problems; their situation weighed heavily on our entire family.

As Pam and I were talking, Jack came outside. He had only met Pam once, but I could tell he didn't like the snippets of conversation he overheard. Jack was characteristically polite to Pam, but she acted noticeably quiet around him.

Jack went back into the house while Pam and I continued talking. She called herself a spirit guide, and even taught seminars on the subject.

Pam explained that my children and I were earthly angels. I listened to her, transfixed; I had never had a conversation about angels before. Pam told me we were all supposed to radiate God's light and love, and that all roads eventually led to God.

Pam's words sounded beautiful to me, and I accepted what she was saying, even when she told me that I was her mother. At that comment a red flag went off in my head, but I continued talking with her.

The next time Jack came back outside, he was visibly upset. I knew I needed to wrap up our discussion, but before Pam left she asked if she could pray for me.

I thought: *Prayer, what could be wrong with that?*

Pam pulled out a keychain with a small plastic teddy bear on the end. While she prayed, she twirled the bear hypnotically around in circles. I have no idea why I didn't stop her, but I didn't. My curiosity got the better of me. I watched her twirl the bear, not paying as much attention to the words she was praying as I should have.

When I finally went inside, I sensed that Jack was unhappy with me. I didn't say much; I wasn't in the mood to get into an argument with him.

As I reflected upon my conversation with Pam, I realized that something had lifted inside of me. I wasn't depressed anymore, and felt a sense of peace I hadn't felt in a long, long time.

The next few days were a whirlwind. I felt like someone was downloading information into my brain. I started thinking non-stop about past lives and reincarnation. Who were Jack and I in our former lives? Who were our friends? Who were our children?

I found the whole topic unbelievable and fascinating at the same time. Pam told me to email her if I was interested in automatic writing, a spiritual practice where I would passively hold a pen and let God take control of my hand, creating words or messages.

Unfortunately, I *was* interested in it.

Past lives. Reincarnation. Automatic writing.

I had never given serious thought to any of these things before I talked to Pam, but now I suddenly knew what I needed to do—I needed to fly to Arizona and share this new knowledge with my family. Surprisingly, Jack was on board with this. He could tell I was happier. I hadn't slipped into a depression after Tim died, which had to be a good thing. Jack was also aware that my brother was going through a rough time, and agreed that it might be a good time for me to go back and visit.

I called my mother and told her I was coming. We decided to surprise my brother and his family. My mother rented two adjacent condominiums at our favorite resort in Scottsdale, and stocked the refrigerator with food in preparation of the long weekend.

The night before I returned home to Hawaii, we were all eating and chatting in the living room. I began telling my family that it was my new understanding that all roads eventually lead to God.

My youngest niece Sandy immediately spoke up.

"No, Aunt Sarah," she said. "You have to go through Jesus to get to the Father."

I stared at my niece. I hadn't thought about Jesus in a long time.

"I used to think that too, Sandy," I told her. "But this way, everyone goes to heaven."

None of the adults in the room said a word.

My other niece, Tessa, spoke up.

"I agree with Aunt Sarah," she said. "My God wouldn't send His children to hell."

Wait. Is that what I said? Confused and exhausted, I excused myself and went to bed.

As I slept, my mother called Jack in Hawaii and told him that something was very wrong with me.

> *If anyone causes one of these little ones—those who believe in me— to stumble, it would be better for them to have a large millstone hung around their neck and to be drowned in the depths of the sea. Woe to the world because of the things that cause people to stumble! Such things must come, but woe to the person through whom they come!*
> *Matthew 18:6-7 NIV*

Upon returning to Hawaii, I continued on my misguided path of "enlightenment," and to my detriment, I didn't give a single thought to the consequences of what I was venturing into. Two days after being home, I woke up to a feeling of pure dread. This feeling was something new and different for me. I walked downstairs, where Jack was getting ready to leave for work.

I sat on the bottom step of the stairs.

"I'm not feeling well today," I told him. "Would you stay home with me?"

"Are you sick?" Jack asked.

"No," I said. "Something just isn't right. I feel like something awful is going to happen."

"That's ridiculous," Jack said. "Nothing awful is going to happen. Anyway... we're busy at work. I'd like to, but I can't stay home with you today."

I didn't know what to say. Jack and I had been married for nearly twenty-four years and I had never asked him to stay home with me. The one time that I did, he told me he couldn't.

The day was every bit as bad as I had anticipated. I began writing in a spiral notebook, page after page of delusional thoughts. I was fully aware that something was wrong, but I had no idea how to fix it. I couldn't think of anyone who could help me.

On some level, I understood that I was going through a spiritual battle. I tried to think of any friends I knew who were religious, but no one came to mind.

Finally, I remembered a school librarian that one of my children had. Norma acted spiritual, and I asked Jack to take me to see her. He agreed, and we drove to her school. When we got there, Jack went into the library to fill Norma in on what was happening to me.

Five minutes later they came out to get me.

Sitting on a small school chair surrounded by books, I told Norma everything I had been through in the past couple of weeks. She listened quietly and patiently, until finally she spoke.

"You need to go home and rest," Norma said. "Is it okay if I visit you tonight?"

"Of course," I said.

Norma smiled and asked if she could speak to Jack alone. Once I was out of earshot, Norma told Jack that she thought I was having a nervous breakdown. She feared for our family, and told Jack not to leave me alone until this passed.

If it didn't pass, she told Jack to take me to our doctor.

Jack and I went home to our kids. Neither Addy, who was in high school, nor Wyatt, who was in third grade, suspected anything.

In anticipation of Norma's visit, I cleaned the house. Our family ate a pleasant dinner together, and then I sent the kids upstairs to do their homework.

When Norma came over, the three of us went outside to talk. Sitting under the bright, beautiful full moon, I remember thinking that everything was going to be alright.

As I finished my thought, Norma put her hand on mine and expressed exactly what I was thinking.

"Everything is going to be alright," she whispered. "I know it is."

CHAPTER 6

That night after Norma left, I was emotionally drained. I climbed into bed and fell fast asleep, hoping I would wake in the morning feeling refreshed... feeling happy... feeling normal.

That is *not* what happened.

In the middle of the night, I awoke to a feeling like something was being sucked into my body. At that same moment, I had a vivid out-of-body experience and clearly saw the terrifying thing that was happening to me.

As I lay comfortably in my bed, a large, dark spirit drifted through our third-floor bedroom window and entered my sleeping body. Strangely, I wasn't afraid. I got out of bed, walked downstairs, and curled up on the end of our living room sofa.

I naively assumed that it was God's spirit that had entered me. After all, I had been thinking about God for weeks, so it *had* to be God, right?

I began communicating with the spirit telepathically, asking it question after question after question. I was in awe, honored that the God of the universe was talking to *me*.

But part of me still needed proof.

"If this is really you, God," I said, "can you make it rain?"

"God doesn't control the weather," the spirit replied. "That's Mother Nature."

Mother Nature?

That didn't sound right, but I decided to let it go.

"If you say so, God," I said.

Our conversation continued from there. It began innocently enough, but the longer the spirit and I talked, the darker our conversation got. The topic switched from the weather to sex pretty quickly.

The spirit confirmed to me everything I'd been thinking and writing about recently. Not just writing, but *automatic writing*, which had been focused on past lives and reincarnation.

During our conversation, the spirit explained to me that our souls travel through time in pods of six, and that the same five souls have been with me since the beginning of humanity.

It told me that the souls that had traveled with me throughout existence were people I knew well… all except one. It explained how, in every new lifetime, the souls were shuffled around and inhabited different bodies.

While in this lifetime I was married to Jack, in the past my soul had been married to someone else in the pod. In this lifetime, that "someone else" was someone I had grown dangerously close to.

Allen.

And that one person in my pod who I didn't know well… Jack did. In fact, Jack and I had had several heated discussions about her, and I felt that he had acted inappropriately with her on more than one occasion.

I found myself agreeing with everything the spirit was saying. Unfortunately, I became so engrossed in the tale it was weaving that I didn't stop to question whether it was actually the One and Only, the Almighty God of the universe.

As I listened, mesmerized, the spirit proceeded to tell me not only that Jack was having an affair with the women from our "pod", but exactly *where* Jack was having this affair.

Oddly, the spirit encouraged his affair, as well as adultery, homosexuality, and divorce for me. For my entire life I had suspected I was bisexual, and although I had never acted on it, I believed what the spirit was saying. My bisexuality had long been my shameful secret. I told the spirit that the Bible said those things were wrong.

"They're not wrong for you," the spirit replied.

When the spirit told me I was special, I believed it.

In my mind, because of Allen, I knew how easily one could justify adultery and divorce. And even though the spirit's words were foreign to me, they also made a strange kind of sense.

Finally, after several grueling, mind-numbing hours, the spirit told me to wake Jack up.

I was beyond exhausted. The spirit had been so methodical that I had fallen for every one of its traps. Even so, I went upstairs and woke Jack up.

Too drained to be angry over what the spirit had told me, I accused Jack of having an affair. I told Jack I knew who he was having the affair with, and even where they met for their rendezvous.

Jack didn't say a word.

Instead, he got out of bed, walked calmly down the stairs, and called my mother in Arizona. All I heard were the words: "You were right, Mom."

That's when the spirit turned evil.

While Jack was still downstairs, the spirit told me that if I didn't do everything it told me to do, it would hurt Jack. Jack came back upstairs and told me to stay in bed; he would get the kids to school.

The spirit told me again that it would hurt Jack, but that was nothing compared to what it would do if I didn't follow its instructions.

With horror, I noticed that Jack was grimacing, holding his side. As he talked to me, I nodded. I felt as if my brain, not my head, was being held hostage by razor, sharp claws. I was too terrified to speak and too weak to move.

After taking the kids to school, Jack came home. He told me to shower, dress, and put my makeup on.

That was odd—Jack didn't care about makeup.

Jack asked me where the rent check was. We owned a rental property, and the renters had just dropped off their monthly check. I had no idea why he wanted it now.

As I undressed to get into the shower, Jack gasped.

"When did you lose all that weight?" he asked.

I didn't know. When I looked in the mirror, I was even surprised at how thin I had gotten over the past few weeks. Thank goodness for showers, I thought, although I wasn't sure if my fear-fueled stench would ever wash off.

After my shower, Jack stayed with me as I dressed and put on my makeup—I wondered if he was worried I would try and run away. That was the furthest thing from my mind, even though I had no idea where Jack was taking me, and was too afraid to ask.

While we were driving, the spirit continued to torment me. It told me that Jack was taking me someplace to be judged.

Judged?

I knew there was nothing to judge. I was guilty. I was a sinner. I was going straight to hell. I had just spoken to our holy, heavenly Father about unspeakable things—sexual things. Adultery. Divorce.

"I'm not just a sinner," I thought. "I'm the worst sinner in the entire world to have talked to God like that."

Jack pulled into our local shopping plaza and parked in a diagonal spot. He got out and walked to the ATM.

The spirit convinced me that Jack was getting money to pay off the person who was going to judge me; although, in reality, he was simply depositing our renter's check.

As Jack stood at the ATM, the spirit continued taunting me. It told me I now had to make a difficult decision. It gave me two choices, both involving Jack and our children.

Neither choice had a good outcome.

In the first scenario, I would kill Jack with a gun that we did not currently own. If I did that, Jack and one of my children would go to heaven. The other two would go to hell. Meanwhile, I would go to prison for the rest of my life.

In the second scenario, if I went to the hospital right now, the outcome would be the same. Jack and one of my children would go to heaven, but the other two would still go to hell. In this case, I would not go to prison.

At this point, I still thought I was communicating with God, and was terrified because I could not make the choice.

The spirit was pressuring me to decide, even though I knew that I couldn't. There *was* no right decision.

I also felt, deep in my soul, that because I would rather die than make a decision that would result in a fate worse than death for my children, I was headed to hell.

In desperation, I called out: "KILL ME, GOD!"

The moment these words left my lips, I had a vision. In

this vision, the single word SAVED flashed in my mind in big, red, bold letters.

Did that just happen?

I didn't know what the word meant, exactly, but I knew it had to be good.

Seconds later, an old pickup truck pulled up next to ours on the right side. On the back window of the cab, in the upper-left corner, was a sticker that contained a single word.

SAVED.

As soon as I read that, I passed out.

> *For our struggle is not against flesh and blood, but against the rulers, against the authorities, against the powers of this dark world and against the spiritual forces of evil in the heavenly realms.*
>
> *Ephesians 6:12 NIV*

❧

When I came to, I found myself in the parking lot of the main hospital on the other side of the island.

Jack was trying to wake me up. A male nurse with a wheelchair stood by my side. I slowly climbed down from the truck into the wheelchair.

It wasn't until I was inside the hospital that I remembered the two choices the spirit had given me.

I had to figure out a way to escape.

Surrounded by hospital employees, I pulled Jack aside.

"You have to get me out of here," I pleaded. "I'm serious, Jack. I can't stay here. Something terrible is going to happen."

I could tell by the look in Jack's eyes that there was no way he was taking me home.

"Please," I continued. "I *have* to get out of here."

As I hugged him, I realized he was trembling, and that his shirt was soaking wet. I looked at his face and noticed how pale he was.

I was not the only one living this nightmare.

I decided to cooperate and not fight the hospital check-in process any longer. Jack was visibly relieved. They monitored my vital signs, took my blood and urine, and gave me an MRI because Jack had told the staff I'd been jogging days before and fallen down. He suggested that I might have hit my head.

The doctors couldn't find anything physically wrong with me, so they placed me in the mental ward. When they found out there were no drugs or alcohol in my system, they prescribed some pills for me to take.

I don't normally even take aspirin, but in this case, I never would have calmed down without medication. Being indwelt by an evil spirit was not only a shameful experience, but a traumatizing one as well.

It was so traumatic, in fact, that I could barely talk about it, even while medicated. I stayed in the hospital for three days so the staff could monitor my mental and physical health while on the medication.

For his part, Jack was scared and exhausted. He didn't know what to think, and at this point he still didn't have any idea what I had experienced. He remembered what Norma had said, and asked the doctor if I might be having a mental breakdown.

The doctor informed him that they don't use that term anymore. He also suggested that my recent trip to Arizona might have triggered something. Perhaps the time change had affected me; everyone handles jet lag differently.

Meanwhile, Jack had a lot of questions.

If I had a mental illness, why was it showing up in my late forties… and how could we not have known about it before?

Did I have severe depression… and if I did, could that have caused the mental illness?

Did I hit my head while jogging … and if I did, why didn't it show up on the MRI?

What exactly was wrong with me?

Over the next few days, the doctor's, whom I spent very little time with, diagnosed me with several mental health disorders. They sent me home with an antipsychotic, and strongly recommended that I see a psychiatrist.

What only God knew was that I had a new perspective and outlook on life. In my own home and vehicle, over the course of eight torturous hours, I had been forever changed.

> Therefore, if anyone is in Christ, the new creation has come: The old has gone, the new is here!
>
> 2 Corinthians 5:17 NIV

CHAPTER 7

My recovery process was extremely slow.

The antipsychotic medication the doctors gave me made me feel as if an elephant was sitting on my chest. Simple tasks like getting my kids to school on time became overly difficult for me.

On top of this, I was riddled with guilt. Why did God allow this to happen to me? What had I done to deserve this?

Along with my guilt came shame. It was mortifying to think I had communicated with a wicked, hateful spirit, believing it was God. I was suspicious at first, but came to believe it really was Him. I thought that only God had the power to communicate with me telepathically. I didn't realize that it wasn't God's spirit I was communicating with until I began reading the Bible they gave me in the hospital. Sadly, I was given little guidance about spiritual matters while there.

I was trying to process several overlapping emotions at once, but curiously, my most overwhelming emotion was *hunger.*

I was insatiably hungry for the Word of God.

Knowing that the word SAVED came from the Bible, and knowing that I had experienced something supernatural, I deduced that the answers to what God had allowed me to experience could only be found in the Bible.

Reading the Bible proved to be very healing for me, but I didn't just read the Bible… I *devoured* it. I became obsessed with Jesus and His Word. The drug I was taking slowed down my body and mind, so I was able to sit and read the Bible for hours at a time.

There are many stories in the Bible of demon possessed people. I related the most to Mary Magdalene, the woman from whom Jesus cleansed of seven demons. Because of that, I believe Mary knew Jesus in an entirely different way than the other disciples did. Mary knew she was different after Jesus cast demons from her-- only God could do that.

Reading the Bible fascinated me. It gave me an entirely new appreciation and understanding of God's Word. The Bible came alive for me, and after researching what SAVED meant in Biblical terms, I fell deeply and utterly in love with Jesus Christ: King of kings, Lord of lords, the Protector and Rescuer of my soul!

For the first time in my life, I understood what *holy* meant—God is holy. God is pure. God is good.

For the first time in my life, I believed that the God of the universe knew me personally. He knew everything I had ever said, thought, or done, including many I was ashamed of, and He loved me anyway!

I knew that because of my sin I did not deserve to be SAVED. I knew that it was only God's grace and mercy that spared me from receiving what I truly deserved.

I knew that with a single word Jesus had SAVED me

from my sin and from the clutches of Satan. I belonged to Him forever and for that, I would be eternally thankful.

> *When evening came, many who were demon-possessed were brought to him, and he drove out the spirits with a word and healed all the sick.*
>
> *Matthew 8:16 NIV*

The hospital recommended that I see a psychiatrist—and because Jack and I had so many unanswered questions, we made an appointment to see one.

Still feeling extremely fragile, I asked the psychiatrist if he had ever spoken to someone who said they had been possessed.

"Yes," he said in a quiet voice, although I could tell he had some doubts.

I hesitated. I didn't see the point of telling my entire story to someone who didn't believe any of it. We stayed, but it was useless.

Over the next few months we visited several other psychiatrists but had the same frustrating experience over and over. Their only answer would be to switch my medication, and as much as I needed the medication I was on, I knew it was not going to be the long-term answer to my situation. I realized then that I had to place my trust not in psychiatrists, but in God.

After all, God knew I had been indwelt by a demon. God knew I had experienced a unique and terrifying form of suffering and torment, and God knew that I was now indwelt by the Holy Spirit.

I didn't have a disease that doctors could cure. For me, psychiatry was at its best an educated guess, but at its worst could cause me grave harm. I needed someone to give me a simple and *Biblical* explanation of why God had allowed a wicked, demonic spirit to inhabit my body for almost eight hours. I considered talking to a pastor, but we weren't attending church at the time, and I didn't want to monopolize anyone's time.

Curiously, I didn't tell Jack about the spirit until after I came home from the hospital. In the hospital, I was in complete shock; I needed to calm down and process the incident before I could verbalize it.

I found myself under an overwhelming amount of mental stress, but Jack and I were determined to find someone who could help me. I requested that Jack attend the appointments with me so he could hear what I had experienced in detail.

It was an exhausting search. Finding a therapist on the island began to seem hopeless since most of the doctors were secular. Finally, I came across a Christian counselor named Rebecca, who was unlike any of the other psychiatrists we had spoken with.

Rebecca told me she had heard of people being controlled by demons, and that there were many instances of demon possession in the Bible. Relieved, I knew that Rebecca had the potential to believe my story.

Talking with Rebecca marked the beginning of my understanding of the true difference between the secular and Christian worlds. Talking with Rebecca allowed me to regain my confidence and my life. Rebecca's therapy was focused on God, and fortunately for me, there was nothing more that I wanted to learn or talk about.

The first thing Rebecca wanted to know was where I stood spiritually. I told her I had been baptized in the

Catholic Church as an infant. As a young girl I remembered going to Sunday school at a Presbyterian church, but only on Easter and Christmas. I faithfully prayed rote, rhyming prayers before dinner and bedtime.

Even now, I still prayed almost every night.

I explained to Rebecca that Jack and I had been married in a Christian wedding ceremony at a friend's church. Shortly afterwards, we received Jesus at a mega church's altar call on the Fourth of July, although we didn't start going to church on a regular basis until Ryan turned two. When Ryan and Addy were young, they were dedicated during a Sunday service at our church in Arizona. I had volunteered many times in the church nursery. We talked about God in our home, and it was important to us that all three of our children attend Christian preschools.

After everything I had been through, one thing that still confused me was I wasn't sure whether I had been a Christian or not before Jesus SAVED me.

Rebecca told me she didn't know either. She explained that only God knows our heart, but that my story sounded to her like the parable of the lost sheep.

Rebecca pulled out her Bible and read it to me:

> Then Jesus told them this parable: "Suppose one of you has a hundred sheep and loses one of them. Doesn't he leave the ninety-nine in the open country and go after the lost sheep until he finds it? And when he finds it, he joyfully puts it on his shoulders and goes home. Then he calls his friends and neighbors together and says, 'Rejoice with me; I have found my lost sheep.' I tell you that

in the same way there will be more rejoicing in heaven over one sinner who repents than over ninety-nine righteous persons who do not need to repent.

Luke 15:3-7 NIV

As I listened to Rebecca read, all I could think about was how undeserving I was of such great love.

CHAPTER 8

The first step to regaining my life was for my family to get back to church which, unfortunately, was easier said than done. Jack and I weren't thrilled with every aspect of our church, so we hadn't attended for a while.

But it was time to go back, so two weeks after I was SAVED, my family humbly made its way back to church. Jack was driving, tapping his foot to the music. I sat in the passenger's seat, writing out our tithe check. Addy and Wyatt were in the back.

I turned around to ask the kids what the date was. They told me, but when I turned back to fill it in, my check pad was gone!

Still fragile from the past couple of weeks, I began to lose it. I searched my purse for the checks. The checkbook cover was there, but the pad of checks had simply disappeared!

I knew then that getting my family to church was even more important than I thought it was. We were still dealing with the demonic, but in faith I believed that God would protect us.

I was slightly afraid I might do something at church to embarrass myself or my family, so I asked Jack if we could sit in the back. Jack didn't know what had happened in the car, but he dutifully found four seats for us at the back of the church.

The service was beautiful. Jack and I both experienced a peace we hadn't felt for quite some time, and I knew we were exactly where we were supposed to be.

That afternoon, still fretting about my missing checks, I went to the garage to search the car. When I felt under the front passenger seat, I found the missing check pad. It had become lodged in the springs, and the check was still filled out. The only thing missing was the date.

A couple of months later, my family was doing its best to return to whatever our new normal looked like—and I did my part by stupidly getting on a balance board and breaking my arm. For various reasons, it was five days before an orthopedic surgeon could perform surgery on me. While I laid in my own bed waiting for surgery, my dear grandmother in Michigan passed away. My sweet grandfather had passed away years before and I was able to say goodbye to him over the phone, but sadly, I wasn't able to do the same with my grandma. Even though my thinking was clouded from the pain and medication I was on, I was thankful that grandma was finally with Jesus and my grandpa.

After my surgery, as I lay in bed reading the Bible and recuperating, I asked the Lord what I was supposed to be learning from this new experience. I had never hurt myself before, and I was struck by the unsettling realization that I was alone. I spoke to my mainland family on the phone and Jack and the kids were thankfully with me, but where were my friends?

I knew they were busy moms like me, but having them not call or come by very often to check on me was not only confusing, but hurtful.

Then it hit me—I had been *purposely* isolating myself from my friends for the past couple of months.

What they didn't know was that my isolation stemmed from the trauma I'd been dealing with since I had been demonically invaded.

It had been months since that horrific experience, and I still hadn't revealed the details of what had happened, even to my closest friends.

Looking woefully at my broken arm, I ultimately realized that my little family was all alone on this small island in the middle of the Pacific Ocean.

During my recuperation, I decided I needed new friends, friends who believed that the Bible was the infallible word of God. Friends for whom Jesus came first in their lives.

I didn't want to abandon my old friends, but I needed some new friends I could talk to about Jesus, friends I could count on in times of trouble. I needed friends who would allow me to be present for *their* trials.

Fortunately, I knew people like that existed at church. Jack and I signed up for a small Bible Study, and there I instantly connected with several mature Christian women. In fact, I met so many women that I had to prayerfully consider which of them I wanted to nurture one-on-one relationships with.

Naturally, everything worked out beautifully, because God had a plan for me, just like He always does.

Shortly after beginning our Bible Study, our church announced the date for its next baptism.

I didn't even have to think about it—it had long been my desire for my family to get baptized together, although because of what had happened the prior year, I *was* willing to get baptized alone.

I called Ryan and told him my plan, and was delighted when he said he'd fly home from school to get baptized with me.

Addy and Jack were on board as well.

The only thing that gave me pause was Wyatt's request to be baptized. He was only nine, and I didn't know if he was ready or not. It was important to me that he understood what he was doing, but when I told him my concern, he started crying.

"But I love Jesus too!" Wyatt said.

I was overjoyed. My dream was coming true, and I had nothing to do with it. God was in full control. The five of us were going to get baptized in the ocean, on one of the most beautiful beaches in the country. It was a miraculous gift to me that all of our hearts were ready at the same time.

The day of the baptism was gorgeous. Twenty-five people were baptized that day. What made it particularly special was that several of the youth pastors who performed the baptism had been involved in Ryan and Addy's teen lives—and would eventually be involved in Wyatt's.

The five of us laughed, cried, and hugged as we publicly confessed our love for Jesus. Afterwards, a church friend walked up to me and said, "You'd better be on guard, because now you're on Satan's radar."

Fortunately, I already knew that.

Then Jesus came to them and said, "All authority in heaven and on earth has been given to me. Therefore go and make disciples of all the nations, baptizing them in the name of the Father and of the Son and of the Holy Spirit, and teaching them to obey everything I have commanded you. And surely I am with you always, to the very end of the age."
Matthew 28:18-20 NIV

CHAPTER 9

Every so often Norma, the librarian friend I had gone to for spiritual guidance, checked in to see how I was healing. When I explained that I was still having anxiety, she reminded me that she practiced reiki, the new-age Japanese technique of using touch to provide healing energy. Norma taught the method of keeping her hands an inch away from the body; the only part of the body she touched was the head.

Norma had first mentioned reiki to me years ago when Addy had pneumonia and was missing a lot of school. Norma wanted to perform reiki on her—but since I didn't know her that well, I declined her offer.

Now that I knew and trusted Norma more, I was more open to the practice. She defined the process as "spiritually guided life force energy work."

Against my better judgment, I agreed to let Norma perform reiki on me. She brought me to a room in her home. I was surrounded by lit, fragrant candles, while quiet meditation music played in the background. I lay down on a massage table, fully clothed, as Norma moved her hands above and over my entire body.

I found it extremely relaxing.

It wasn't until several strange incidents occurred that I questioned why I allowed Norma to perform reiki on me. I didn't even understand what it actually was. Was it really energy work or healing?

One night I was awakened by a buzzing sound. After getting out of bed and turning on the light, I realized the sound was surrounding my bed. I couldn't see or feel anything, but I could hear the loud buzzing sound clearly in my ears.

It occurred to me that I should pray—and when I did, the sound went away. The next morning I researched the dangers of reiki, and discovered that several religions considered it demonic.

Ashamed that I had once again allowed something dark into my life, I stopped reiki immediately.

<hr />

Shortly after our family was baptized, I woke up one morning confused and angry with Jack. I was still dealing with the trauma of having been demonically indwelt, and I realized that the spirit had told me a few truths among its many lies.

One of the accusations I couldn't shake was that of Jack being unfaithful to me. I had known and loved him since high school, and I didn't believe he was capable of cheating on me. I considered him to be one of the most noble and honest human beings I had ever known.

The spirit, however, was so convincing about Jack's infidelity that it continued to haunt me. I confronted him again and, when pressed, he admitted that he had been unfaithful to me during the early years of our marriage.

Not surprisingly, I did not deal with this well. My life already contained more stress than I could handle, so I responded by completely shutting down.

Jack and I still had two children living at home and, being a child of divorce myself; I resolved to keep my marriage together at all costs. Jack had long ago forgiven me for having feelings for another man. I was going to do my best to forgive him for being unfaithful. Consciously or subconsciously, I did *just enough* to keep Jack from walking away.

At times I didn't act like a Christian. At times, even though I was in love with Jesus and SAVED, I was shocked by the words that came out of my mouth. I couldn't have described the depth of my pain even if someone had asked me to. It was a *physical* pain, and along with the pain came questions.

Who was this person I was married to? How insidious had his infidelity been to our marriage?

I didn't know what was true and what was false. Nothing made sense to me anymore.

Jack and I began seeing a marriage counselor, to no avail. No one could tell us how to repair broken trust. And it didn't feel just broken, but annihilated.

Jack could have told me it was snowing out when it was, and I wouldn't have believed him. A friend of ours urged us to pray together. We did, but I had mixed emotions as we did so. Part of me was skeptical of what I was hearing. The other part liked listening to what was on Jack's heart, even if I didn't always believe what he was saying.

I regretted that we hadn't prayed together as newlyweds. Would that have made a difference? What if, when Jack and I received Jesus in 1984 on the Fourth of July, someone had offered to teach us about God? In reality, several years passed after our altar call before we even walked back into a church.

We simply didn't know what we didn't know.

So, how do you repair a decades-long marriage that's been rocked to its foundation? Jack and I didn't have the answer, but we *did* decide to stay committed to our family and to God. He was the one to whom we made our marriage vow in 1982, and He was the one who had blessed and protected us all these years... even when we weren't aware of it.

To say that Jack and I had a few rocky years of marriage after that was an understatement. We were obviously struggling and decided it was time to tell our two oldest children what we were dealing with. As difficult as it was to tell Addy and Ryan about our situation, at least they knew the truth. Our secrets were creating misguided assumptions and confusion and we already had enough of that.

I told our youngest son last. Wyatt was in his late teens, and one day after church, he begged me to explain how I could be so on fire for the Lord, yet sometimes so cold to his father. Feeling as if I had no other choice, I told him the truth.

A couple of hours after I told him, Wyatt told me it was the best gift I could have given him.

Eventually, Jack and I ended up leading separate lives, albeit in the same house. We were both serving our community and all of our kids seemed happy, so we just kept doing what worked for us. I started taking classes at the local community college and helping out at our church.

One night, during a mid-week Bible Study, I realized I was feeling some residual effects from the reiki I had ignorantly practiced the year before. Our pastor was talking about the occult, and I now considered reiki to be part of that. Even though I didn't practice it any longer, I still asked around, but no one could tell me what "energy work" really was.

As my pastor was talking, I was reminded of something strange that both Wyatt and I had experienced before I quit reiki. During one of my community college classes, the professor said something that I thought was funny, and I started to laugh.

Once I started to laugh, I couldn't stop; and when I say I *couldn't* stop, I mean that in a very literal way.

There I was, a middle-aged woman, surrounded by twenty year old students, and I was having a laughing fit. It was humiliating, and I had to leave the classroom to calm down.

Minutes later, I returned to the classroom… only to start laughing again. I apologized to the professor and the class and, oddly enough, told them I had just come from a reiki session.

"Now I understand," the professor said.

That experience was so embarrassing that I wanted to drop the course, but I didn't. Regrettably, I never asked my teacher what she meant by her statement, or what she thought of reiki.

The following week, Wyatt's teacher called to tell me he had had a laughing fit at school; she said she'd never witnessed anything like it before.

I hung up with his teacher, perplexed. Wyatt and I had both had laughing fits, a few days apart—how strange that we'd both do something so random and bizarre. Was it a coincidence?

During our Bible Study, I realized that the common denominator had to be reiki. Norma had performed it on me, and I had in turn performed it on Wyatt.

That night, I was filled with intense remorse over my past involvement with reiki. After our study, I took my pastor and assistant pastor aside and asked for prayer. We prayed together, then went home.

When Wyatt was in bed, I told him what I had learned in Bible study that night. I told him that I had no business practicing reiki on him since I had absolutely no idea what I was doing.

I asked Wyatt for forgiveness. He forgave me, and we prayed together before he went to sleep.

Leaving Wyatt's room, I knew I had to apologize to Jack as well, as I had also performed reiki on him. I lay down in the bed with him and told him the whole story. As I'd done with Wyatt, I asked him for forgiveness and we prayed.

When Jack and I finished praying, I felt a sensation I had never felt before, like thousands of butterflies were leaving my body.

The sensation lasted three or four very long, terrifying seconds. I thought that I was dying, and that my soul was leaving my body in bits and pieces.

I looked at Jack and screamed for him to help me. He looked at me with a "now what?" face. He didn't have a clue what to do—fortunately, the sensation soon stopped.

That Sunday, I told my pastor what had happened. He said that he had heard of demons resting on people's bodies, making them feel as if they were coming through the skin.

He told me not to worry. I was SAVED. I was sealed by the Holy Spirit. Even though I didn't completely understand what had happened, I trusted what my pastor told me. His words gave me peace.

I continued to research evil spirits in the Bible and realized that by allowing reiki into my life in prior years, I hadn't kept my temple pure.

> "When an impure spirit comes out of a person, it goes through arid places seeking rest and does not find it. Then it says, 'I will return to the house I left.' When it arrives, it finds the house swept clean and put in order. Then it goes and takes seven other spirits more wicked than itself, and they go in and live there. And the final condition of that person is worse than the first."
>
> Luke 11:24-26 NIV

After Jesus cast the demon from me and filled me with the Holy Spirit, it was my responsibility to read God's Word, put it into practice, and be obedient to it. Because I was SAVED and had a relationship with Christ, I wasn't demonized again, but I believe that because of reiki, I had been demonically oppressed. Confession, repentance and obedience broke that oppression.

That was over a decade ago, and I consider it a miracle that there has been no obvious demonic activity since.

> Dear friends, do not believe every spirit, but test the spirits to see whether they are from God, because many false prophets have gone out into the world. This is how you can recognize the Spirit of God: Every spirit that acknowledges that Jesus Christ has come in

the flesh is from God, but every spirit that does not acknowledge Jesus is not from God. This is the spirit of the antichrist, which you have heard is coming and even now is already in the world.

1 John 4:1-3 NIV

CHAPTER 10

I am a born-again Christian.

We are often told in the Christian community that the *born-again* label is a turnoff to unbelievers, but how can you deny who you are? To be born again means to be born from above. It's a spiritual transformation in which one becomes an eternal child of God by trusting in the name of Jesus Christ.

In my case, I had experienced a religious conversion, and God had given me a new belief system—one completely different from what I had previously believed.

I was born again.

To be born again meant that I was not the same person I was before I was SAVED. Never in my forty-six years of life did I think I needed to become a different person. I was happy with who I was. I was proud of who I was. It never occurred to me that I should change my personality or my values. It was never on my radar... but it *was* on God's radar.

God is love, but I have also experienced God's extreme discipline. God will do *what He needs to do to bring* His children to salvation and home to live with Him for eternity.

I wish that I had been SAVED in a gentler way, but that wasn't God's plan for me. Even before I was born, He knew exactly what my life was going to look like, and the various paths I would take to get there.

Even before I was born, He knew that I would not die the woman I was before salvation.

> *The fear of the LORD is the beginning of wisdom; all who follow his precepts have good understanding. To him belongs eternal praise.*
>
> *Psalm 111:10 NIV*

It was my fear and reverence of the Lord that gave me the desire to know and do my best to fulfill His commandments.

It is my prayer that I never disrespect the Lord again. I am completely awed by our God. There was a time shortly after I was SAVED that my guilt over who I had been *before* salvation almost consumed me. I had been so prideful, so ignorant, and so hypocritical. The problem was that I wasn't giving myself grace over the ignorant part.

When I realized that I had just been going through the motions in life, and not understanding or enjoying a relationship with Jesus the way I should have, I couldn't handle the revelation. Because no one had ever explained to me what a relationship with Jesus Christ looked like, I had absolutely no idea I was doing anything wrong. I had absolutely no idea what I was missing out on.

At one point, my guilt became debilitating. My pastor was away on a trip, so I called a church on the other side of the island and explained my concerns to the assistant pastor.

After listening to me, he asked me if I was Catholic.

He said that Catholics were notorious for feeling guilty. I told him that I had been baptized in a Catholic church as an infant, but that I had always attended non-denominational, Bible-based churches.

The pastor explained to me that if I had prayed and truly repented for my sins, God had forgiven them. If I did not believe that was true, I was putting myself and my guilt *above* God and His Word.

That was the last thing I wanted to do.

After some continued discussion, we said our goodbyes and I folded my hands to pray. I thanked God for SAVING me, and then repented for every wrong thing I could think of.

My guilt vanished.

I decided to lay everything at Jesus' feet, and not only to believe that I was forgiven, but to believe that God, in His forgiveness, had decided to erase my sins—after all, that's what the Bible tells us.

Part of my hunger in knowing God's Word was that I still needed to know what I did that made me susceptible to being demon indwelt. Then, once I found out, I needed to change that behavior. I knew that I couldn't truly repent unless I was aware of my sin.

I learned that sanctification—being set apart and made holy—was a process. It was a process, but I wanted to achieve it as quickly as possible.

I knew that I would *never* go back to my old ways.

The Bible tells us that we are capable of taking every thought captive—and while I believed that God heard me when I prayed silently, it had never occurred to me that he "hears" our nasty thoughts as well.

After I was SAVED, I didn't have nearly as many bad thoughts as before—but I didn't want any. I imagined that I had a windshield wiper in my brain, and every time

I started thinking something negative, and every time Satan put an evil thought in my mind, I would wipe it away. This worked for me, and it continues to work. These days I rarely have bad thoughts that need wiping away. Praise God!

⁂

Or do you not know that wrongdoers will not inherit the kingdom of God? Do not be deceived: Neither the sexually immoral nor idolaters nor adulterers nor men who have sex with men nor thieves nor the greedy nor drunkards nor slanderers nor swindlers will inherit the kingdom of God. And that is what some of you were. But you were washed, you were sanctified, you were justified in the name of the Lord Jesus Christ and by the Spirit of our God.

1 Corinthians 6:9-11 NIV

What greater miracle could we ask for than to be cleansed of all the filth we've accumulated in life, and start over with a clean slate? The fundamental change in my disposition is the reason I know my story is true—not a nightmare, not mental illness, not a psychotic episode.

After I was SAVED, God supernaturally gave me a new nature that was clean and pure. There was now no question that I was a heterosexual, married Christian woman. That was who God intended me to be, and that was all that I desired. Never again was there any thought of me being an adulterous, bisexual woman, which was important to me because I had resigned myself to the fact that that was my personal cross to bear.

After I became SAVED, I knew that the Holy Spirit was doing a mighty work in me. Much of my former life had vanished. It was gone. I was walking in the Spirit before I even understood what that meant.

> So I say, walk by the Spirit, and you will not gratify the desires of the flesh. For the flesh desires what is contrary to the Spirit, and the Spirit what is contrary to the flesh. They are in conflict with each other, so that you are not to do whatever you want. But if you are led by the Spirit, you are not under the law.
>
> The acts of the flesh are obvious: sexual immorality, impurity and debauchery; idolatry and witchcraft; hatred, discord, jealousy, fits of rage, selfish ambition, dissensions, factions and envy; drunkenness, orgies, and the like. I warn you, as I did before, that those who live like this will not inherit the kingdom of God.
>
> Galatians 5:16-21 NIV

As a Christian, I knew that I was still going to sin, but I wasn't going to continue *living* in sin. Purity was something I had never experienced before. Growing up, one of our relatives had adult magazines in their home. I remember my little brother, John and me, being as young as five and six years old looking at them.

They were stacked under the television in plain sight. It was pornography, and sadly, those magazines contaminated our innocent, young minds.

Purity is not something I take for granted. It is something that only I can feel, and something that only He, The Almighty One, could do. I cherish it. The Holy Spirit is slowly transforming me to be like Christ. This is His goal for all of us. God's grace and mercy is restoring me to His original design. After I was SAVED, I literally felt as if I were starting over... and I was. I had been converted.

The process has taken longer than I thought, but I have come to realize that to have a relationship with the Lord, we don't just come to know and love Him through His Word. We come to know and love Him through our *obedience*. There is joy in knowing we are doing the right thing by being obedient to the Creator of the Universe.

Then there are the blessings, which come in all forms. For example, God doesn't want us to be anxious or to worry. According to the Bible, worry itself is a sin.

When I started having stomach issues my counselor, Rebecca, suggested I was probably dealing with Post Traumatic Stress Disorder (PTSD). Of course I had PTSD. Why hadn't I thought of that myself? I had so many of the symptoms, and was becoming increasingly unhealthy.

"Stress kills," Rebecca simply stated.

The more I researched my condition, the more I decided to actively lead a healthy, peaceful lifestyle. That was not going to be easy. I was going to have to deal with worry, anxiety, PTSD, and triggers.

I took all of those things and placed them at Jesus' feet.

I've learned to pray when I'm worried or anxious—and God blesses me for it. He replaces that worry or anxiety with His supernatural peace that surpasses all understanding.

Some of the other gifts resulting from this peace are that I am physically stronger, calmer, and healthier. Rebecca taught me a multitude of ways to relax, and what self care is all about.

She helped immensely, but it was God's Word that is healing me.

> "Therefore I tell you, do not worry about your life, what you will eat or drink; or about your body, what you will wear. Is not life more than food, and the body more than clothes? Look at the birds of the air; they do not sow or reap or store away in barns, and yet your heavenly Father feeds them. Are you not much more valuable than they? Can any one of you by worrying add a single hour to your life?
>
> Matthew 6:25-27 NIV

The following stories are a collection of some of the experiences and miracles that I have received from God. I am grateful for them in countless ways, but mostly because they have drawn me closer to the Lord, and have been instrumental to my healing process.

CHAPTER 11

Have I not commanded you? Be strong and courageous. Do not be afraid; do not be discouraged, for the LORD your God will be with you wherever you go."

Joshua 1:9 NIV

The moment my son Ryan was born, my life changed for the better.

The minute I held him in my arms, I understood what unconditional love was. God rocked my world with that child, and before I knew it he was grown up and headed to college.

College, too, passed by in the blink of an eye.

After Ryan graduated, he planned to travel to China to teach English. Jack and I agreed at first, but the closer he came to leaving, the more nervous I got. Right before he signed his employment contract, I told Ryan how I was feeling.

To my astonishment, he told me he wouldn't go.

"Just like that?" I asked him.

"Yes, mom," Ryan said. "I love you, and don't want you to worry."

Instead, Ryan went to Europe to mirror his sister Addy, who was studying abroad in France.

Ryan and Addy were three years apart and had a very close relationship. They had many friends in common, so it was no surprise that Ryan wanted to go to France with his sister. It was such a simple solution, I couldn't believe I hadn't come up with it.

They had an amazing time, and when Ryan got back, he told us he intended to return to France and study photography. To make that happen, he lived with us in Hawaii and worked two jobs for the year. I was happy to have him back, and spent every minute I could with him before he left again.

Before heading back to France, Ryan decided to stop in Arizona and visit our family for a couple of days.

Two days after Ryan left, something very unusual happened to Wyatt and me.

On an otherwise ordinary day, I picked Wyatt up from school and took him to the grocery store. There was a parking space by the front door of the store, so we quickly ran in, grabbed a few groceries, and ran out.

When I opened the driver's-side door of our old SUV, the alarm started blaring. I jumped; I didn't even know our car *had* an alarm.

Each time the grocery store door opened, a dozen people stared at us. I frantically pushed buttons on my keys and on the dashboard, but nothing worked.

Embarrassed that I couldn't figure out how to stop the alarm, I asked Wyatt to call his dad and prepare him for what was coming home. We drove all the way there with the alarm blaring.

Jack met us on the street in front of our house. He jumped into the SUV and pulled out the owner's manual. We drove to an isolated parking lot so we wouldn't bother the neighbors. Eventually, Jack figured out how to turn the alarm off. The whole thing was surprising considering that we'd owned the SUV for several years and nothing like that had ever happened.

That evening, Ryan FaceTimed us from my mother and stepfather's house in Phoenix. He told us he had a funny story he wanted to share with us.

Ryan had borrowed his grandfather's car to visit his cousin twenty minutes away. When he arrived and got out of the car, the alarm started going off! Ryan pulled out the owner's manual, but couldn't figure out how to turn it off. He called his grandfather, but he had no idea how to turn it off either.

Nothing my stepfather suggested stopped the alarm, so he finally decided to drive over and look at it himself. When he got there, he decided to disconnect the alarm he didn't even know he had, which had been blaring for over an hour.

Jack, Wyatt, and I listened to his story wide-eyed. We were speechless.

"What's wrong with you guys?" Ryan asked.

"The exact same thing happened to us today," I said.

It was their turn to be speechless.

We told Ryan and my parents the story about our SUV. Addy had driven that vehicle for five years and, like us, didn't even know it had an alarm.

Stunned, the six of us sat there, wondering what all of it meant.

Because I hadn't been thrilled about the idea of Ryan going back to France by himself in the first place, I thought that perhaps the alarm signaled danger—meaning that Ryan shouldn't be going!

Fortunately, I held my tongue and didn't say anything along those lines.

After our call, Jack and I talked at length about coincidences, divine appointments and spiritual warfare.

For a few minutes, I let my fear take over, until I remembered that fear is not from the Lord. Fear is a tool that Satan uses. I had allowed fear to take over when Ryan wanted to go to China, and I didn't want to do that to him again.

In faith, I decided to turn what Satan had planned for evil into something good. God was with us; it didn't matter how far away Ryan was while he was at school. God would be with him. God would protect him.

Knowing that was a huge comfort for me. It would have been easy for me to beg Ryan not to go to France because of the "scary" sign of the car alarms going off.

Once again, I had to choose to trust in God, knowing that He is where my strength comes from.

Ryan arrived safely at school and had a wonderful experience. The following year, we all traveled over for his graduation. Our family spent three dreamlike weeks in France and Italy; both countries were even more wonderful than we expected them to be. The five of us had always traveled well together; but this trip was different. Our family had been through a lot over the past several years, and this was a time of healing, of just being with one another safe and content, of love.

God knew what our precious family needed, and that's exactly what He gave us.

Before we traveled to Europe, Ryan had decided that he

wasn't moving back to Hawaii after graduation. He wanted to get started on his photography career, and the best place to do that for him was New York City. A friend of Ryan's had generously invited Ryan to live with him while he got settled.

Ryan was planning on leaving Paris two days after us, and we didn't know when we would see him again.

When the taxi arrived to take us to the airport, I could hardly say goodbye. The five of us had shared an unforgettable European holiday, but Ryan wasn't coming home with us. Jack and I were both sobbing as we got into the taxi.

Within a week, Ryan had moved to Brooklyn and was working in Manhattan. I FaceTimed Ryan and told him about Jack and I crying all the way to the airport.

"I did the same thing," Ryan told me.

That surprised me—Ryan wasn't a big crier.

"Why were *you* crying?" I asked.

"I met someone," Ryan said.

My heart dropped.

"What do you mean, you met someone?" I asked.

Not once in the past four weeks had Ryan mentioned he was dating anyone. He seemed fully present with us, not preoccupied at all.

"Mom, I love you," Ryan said, "and I knew it would ruin your vacation if I told you about her."

My heart dropped further.

"Why?" I asked. "Is she from France?"

"No," Ryan said. "She's from Brazil."

Once again, I struggled not to say anything I'd regret, doing my best not to let fear take over. I asked Ryan about his girlfriend. Because truth is always the best policy, I wished he hadn't kept his secret from us. Knowing about her wouldn't have ruined my trip, but Ryan was correct—it would have *changed* our trip. His long-distance relationship would have been on my mind constantly.

I would have worked through it though, and come to the same conclusion I always did—that God is in control and everything He does is for the good of those that love Him.

Six months later, we met our future daughter-in-law, Juliana, when she and Ryan came to Hawaii for a visit.

We instantly fell in love with her. The following year she moved to New York, and two years after that she and Ryan got married by a justice of the peace, with eventual plans of having a celebration of their marriage in Brazil.

God has blessed the two of them in marvelous ways, but I can't help but think that none of it ever would have happened if we had let fear take over the day the car alarms went off.

CHAPTER 12

*They triumphed over him by the blood of the
Lamb and by the word of their testimony;
they did not love their lives so much as to
shrink from death.*

Revelation 12:11 NIV

There was a young woman at our church named
Megan; she was a very thoughtful and social
mother of twin boys. Megan approached our pastor
about starting a ministry for mothers of preschoolers. She
had run a similar program at her old church, and it had been
a huge success.

Our pastor loved the idea, and asked me if I'd be part
of it.

This was a big step for me.

I told him—cautiously—that I'd help Megan get the
program started. A typical Monday morning consisted
of breakfast, crafts, a speaker, fellowship—and, most
importantly, child care!

Megan's program was a big hit. Many of the mothers

told us that Monday mornings were the highlight of their week.

At the end of the year, our group held a banquet that Megan gleefully called "Tea and Testimony." She casually asked me if I'd be willing to share my testimony with the other mothers.

I froze.

Megan asked me again.

"I don't think so," I stammered. "My testimony is pretty *out there*."

Megan laughed.

"I've heard difficult testimonies all my life," she said.

"I don't think you've ever heard one like mine," I assured her. "How about if I type it out and email it to you. You can decide if it's appropriate for the other moms or not."

"Agreed," Megan said. She gave me an encouraging hug and we both headed home.

It finally happened; I always knew it would, and here it was. Someone had finally asked me to give my testimony.

When I got home, I told Jack I needed to rest a bit. I excused myself to our bedroom, curled up in my bed, and thought about what Megan was asking me to do.

She was asking me to tell other people about my conversion.

Only a handful of people knew about my conversion—most of them therapists. I still hadn't told my best friends. Although several people had asked me in the past five years what was "different" about me, I generally gave them the generic response, "I've been born again."

Surprisingly, no one but Megan had ever asked me *how* I became born again.

I took a short nap. When I woke up, I grabbed a pad of yellow paper and my favorite pen, and began to write.

As I wrote out my testimony, I discovered that I felt a tremendous amount of healing and power when I wrote things down. The perspective I gained was life-changing.

However, as I read over what I'd written, I shamefully realized how much of the occult I had dabbled in… and not just the Ouija boards and seances that the neighbor kids and I messed around with in my basement. I'm talking about "grown-up" things like palm readers and hypnotists. I'm talking about opening the newspaper every morning to read my horoscope, about having my tarot cards read, and calling a psychic hotline. I'm talking about yoga, reiki and automatic writing. I even took my daughter, Addy, to see a Kahuna. (Hawaiian shaman)

I believe the final straw for God came when I sat down for several hours with Pam, the neighbor who called herself a spirit guide. I had come to understand that she was really a medium and that the Bible condemns that practice. The Bible condemns all of it.

I'm talking about *sin*.

Reading over my testimony, I was overwhelmed by how "lost" I had been. And I couldn't even claim ignorance because on several occasions, I wouldn't allow my own children to have their tarot cards read or be hypnotized. On some level I knew these things were wrong… but I did them anyway.

Sin craves sin. I was a seeker, and nothing satisfied my craving. I always had to know more. I then realized what my greatest sin had been all of those years.

Unbelief.

I thought that I believed in God, but I also remembered telling a friend, "I believe in everything," which I now know means that I didn't believe in anything.

Megan had asked me to give a fifteen-minute testimony,

but I felt as if I could have talked for hours. Writing out my testimony consumed my life. When I wasn't writing it, I was thinking about it.

After ten days, I had what I thought were enough details to get my story across—hopefully, without scaring all those young mothers to death.

With trepidation, I emailed it to Megan, assuring her for the tenth time that my feelings would not be hurt if she decided not to include my testimony at the Tea and Testimony.

I had done my job; the decision was up to her.

Several days passed, and I heard nothing at all from Megan. I felt vulnerable and exposed. I called my pastor's wife, explained the situation, and asked if I could email her my testimony. I told her to eliminate anything she thought might be too disturbing for our young mothers.

She read it over, then emailed me and Megan, saying that this was my testimony, and that I should share as much of it as I was comfortable sharing.

In other words, it was up to me.

On the morning of the Tea and Testimony, I couldn't stop crying. I was overwhelmed with gut-wrenching, almost debilitating fear. I woke up crying. I cried drinking my coffee. I cried while taking my shower. I cried getting dressed and trying to put my makeup on. I was crying on my way to church when I realized it was raining so hard that I could barely see out my front windshield.

I remembered back to my night with the spirit, when I originally thought I was talking with God. I had asked the spirit to make it rain; it said it couldn't, that only Mother Nature could make it rain.

I realized that God was putting that memory in my mind so that I would understand that everything happens in His timing, not ours.

God was making it rain, and I knew that I was not alone. God was with me. He was making it rain on His terms, and strengthening my heart at the same time.

Instantly, I felt like a warrior heading into battle. I knew that only Jesus SAVES, that I was sealed with the Holy Spirit, and that the God of the Universe was making it rain.

I knew that I was right where I was supposed to be.

I felt prepared but emotionally exhausted. When I arrived at church I greeted everyone in the lobby. A friend of mine had just returned from vacation.

"It's funny how when you get back from vacation, everyone looks so tired," she said.

"Trust me," I laughed. "I don't just look tired. I *am* tired."

Three ladies gave their sweet testimonies before me. All three of them had grown up in the church, all three of them had gone through struggles, and all three of them gave God the glory for where they were in life.

And then there was me.

I felt like a hot mess, weary from thinking and writing about my testimony for nearly two weeks. I was worn out from crying all morning long.

I felt like I was going to slime these beautiful, innocent, unsuspecting mothers with the most horrible story they had ever heard.

My courage seemed to vanish. The warrior in me seemed to melt away. I suddenly felt all alone, just them and me.

I had typed out my testimony, thinking that would be the easiest way to present my story. I went to grab my reading glasses from my purse… but couldn't find them. I had put them in my purse before I left the house. I knew I had.

I kept searching as fear began to creep in. I didn't know if it was Satan or God who had taken my glasses.

After praying a silent prayer, God put it on my heart just to be real, and to tell those moms my story without reading it. I had almost memorized it anyway, and hopefully, no one was expecting perfection.

We were all just moms, after all, telling our "Come to Jesus" stories to each other.

I pulled a chair onto the stage and lowered the microphone. I was worried that I might faint.

I began to speak. Looking at their kind, eager faces, I began to relax and calmly tell the story I had written over the past two weeks. I told these young mothers things I had done… and things I hoped they would never try.

I felt vulnerable on that stage, but protected at the same time. I felt a strength in me that was not my own. I could not have given that testimony by myself. I could not have soldiered on, feeling so exposed.

I was truly letting go, and letting God take over.

I was glad that I hadn't panicked when I couldn't find my reading glasses. I was glad that even though my courage had come and gone all morning, I was continuing to learn to trust in Christ.

Knowing Jesus gave me a strength I never knew I had.

There was one unfamiliar face in the crowd that caught my eye. As I spoke, she kept nodding her head and prodding me on. She encouraged me just by being there.

When I came to the part about the spirit, I decided not to go into further detail when I saw one of the young mothers gasp and put a hand to her mouth.

When I finished speaking, no one said a word. They said NOTHING.

After a long and awkward pause, I decided to break the ice myself. I mumbled something about how wonderful the volunteer babysitters were upstairs. Megan took the hint and closed our group in prayer.

I wanted to run to my car and drive home, but something made me stay. We quietly cleaned up the meeting room, all of us lost in our own thoughts.

My mind was reeling. Several of my friends told me they didn't have any idea I had gone through all of that.

On some level, I knew that my life had just changed. I didn't know how, but it didn't matter—I had been obedient to the Lord and given my testimony.

As I was leaving the church, the encouraging new mom was standing outside, watching her two-year-old climb on a low lava rock wall.

Her name was Perri, and we started talking. She told me that her family had lived on the Big Island years ago, but had recently moved back from the mainland. We chatted for a few minutes, and as I walked away, I knew I'd made a new friend.

When I got home, I emptied my purse, remembering what had happened to my pad of checks on our first Sunday back to church so many years before.

I wasn't surprised to find my reading glasses, right where they were supposed to be.

CHAPTER 13

As iron sharpens iron, so one person sharpens another.

Proverbs 27:17 NIV

The more Perri and I got to know each other, the more I realized what was missing in my life—a friend who loved Jesus as much as I did! A friend I could talk to about Jesus who *wouldn't* think I was odd for being obsessed with Him.

For me, Perri became that friend.

There were many other people at church who were equally "on fire" for Jesus, but Perri and I were on the same page in many other areas as well. We were constantly learning from one another, and I always walked away from our conversations feeling energized and enriched.

One of the things I liked the most about Perri was that she asked me challenging questions that no one else dared, cared, or thought to ask.

When I gave my testimony at church in front of the young mothers, I purposely didn't tell the entire story—I simply said that a spirit came to me, but even that seemed too much for some of the young women listening.

Perri, on the other hand, wanted to know more.

She had come from a mega church on the mainland where they frequently talked about demonic attacks and the spiritual realm. She didn't understand why believers weren't more open to talking about such things.

Perri and I were walking along the beach one day when she asked me to explain more about my experience. With some apprehension, I told Perri *everything* that had happened to me.

I had believed for years that people would shun me once they heard my story, but not Perri. She was surprised by what I told her, but not shocked. Perri had heard many different testimonies, and knew her Bible well.

After that, Perri and I got together often to pray for our families. God was answering our prayers in such powerful ways, that we decided to start a group at our church for mothers who wanted to commit to praying for their children on a regular basis. Once we began praying together, I was able to hear the hearts desires of other Christian mothers.

One of the most difficult parts for me about being born again at forty-six years old, was learning not to regret the past. Thinking about some of my past mistakes as a mother, I desperately wished that Jack and I would have parented our children differently. I felt in many ways we had made our children our idols. Before I was SAVED our world revolved around them, when it should have revolved around God, and helping our children to develop a relationship with Him.

Thankfully, God reminded me of His perfect timing, and I knew that I could pray to Him about anything... even my regrets.

*Do not be anxious about anything, but in
every situation, by prayer and petition, with
thanksgiving, present your requests to God.*
Philippians 4:6 NIV

One Sunday morning, our pastor announced the date for the next church baptism. Listening to him describe the importance of baptism, I realized I had been slightly disappointed in my own family's baptism a few years earlier. That whole day should have been an enormous celebration with our church family—unfortunately, because we hadn't made any plans afterwards, it felt a little bit anticlimactic.

After church, I told the assistant pastor I thought it would be a good idea if the church threw a barbecue after the baptism.

"We've never had one before," he told me. "But go for it!"

Wait, what just happened here?

Realizing I had just been volunteered, I happily arranged for the food, tent, and tables. Our worship leader provided the music. On the morning of the baptism, I dropped Ryan off at the beach to save a picnic space for us. I then headed to the store to buy him coffee and breakfast.

My total bill came to $7.77. Many people consider seven to be God's number, and 777 to represent the threefold perfection of the Trinity.

"You should go to Vegas," the cashier suggested.

I laughed.

"Or maybe a baptism," I said.

The poor cashier had no idea what I was talking about, but I knew that God was pleased.

Before the baptism, while a handful of us were preparing

for the barbecue, I realized that we didn't have nearly enough food or drinks for the people there. I mentioned this to the pastor's wife.

"Don't worry, Sarah," she assured me. "God will provide."

She was right, of course. Our church family had a marvelous afternoon, we ended up with more food and drink than we needed, and people stayed for hours, fellowshipping with one another and listening to music.

It was an afternoon my friends and I will never forget—and I pray the same can be said for the people who were baptized that day.

> So in Christ Jesus you are all children of God through faith, for all of you who were baptized into Christ have clothed yourselves with Christ.
>
> Galatians 3:26-27 NIV

CHAPTER 14

For the creation waits in eager expectation
for the children of God to be revealed.
                                    Romans 8:19 NIV

When people think about "signs" from God, they often imagine something dramatic and miraculous—and sometimes it is. But in my experience, God is often more subtle, speaking to us with something as simple as a ladybug or as serene as a shooting star.

One of the most important things we can do in this life is pour our heart and soul into the lives of the children around us to help them learn who God is. That's one reason why teaching Sunday school is one of the joys of my life!

One morning as I was preparing to teach my Sunday school lesson, I was hanging out with Trey, our worship leader's five-year-old son. We were sitting on a picnic table next to the ocean, waiting for the other children to arrive.

I gave Trey some paper and crayons and asked him to draw me a picture, but he had no idea what to draw.

"How about drawing me a ladybug," I suggested.

"I don't know what they look like," Trey said. "I've never seen one before."

Trey was a little guy, so I didn't think it was too strange that he had never seen a ladybug before. We left the table to look at the sea turtles by the rocks in the ocean.

When we came back to the picnic table, there, sitting motionless on his blank piece of paper, was a ladybug.

"This is what a ladybug looks like," I told him excitedly.

"How'd you do that?" he laughed.

"I didn't do that, Trey," I said. "God did."

❧

I have had the misfortune to know many friends with parents who have Alzheimer's or dementia. My friend Julie's mother passed away after almost a decade of being afflicted with that horrible disease. In the wake of her death, Julie and I occasionally walked down to a bay close to my home, where we would talk and pray for hours.

One night as we were talking, a couple of months after her mother passed, I saw a low-flying shooting star zoom past Julie's head.

Delighted, I asked Julie if she saw it, but of course she didn't because her back was to it. I sat there thinking that it was different than any other shooting star I'd ever seen, so obviously God wanted me to see it.

Should it mean something to me? Was it *my* shooting star? I couldn't think of any specific reason why God would send me my own shooting star, so I decided simply to revel in the magic of what I had witnessed.

Julie turned her chair in the direction the star had fallen. "I have to tell you a story," she said.

Julie proceeded to tell me about how she had recently been walking her precious old golden retriever at the park by her house, praying to God for a sign about her mother. Lying on her back on the cool, green grass, her loving dog by her side, Julie asked God for a shooting star. She waited patiently, and when she didn't see a shooting star, she continued on home.

That was the answer to my question. No wonder I couldn't claim that shooting star as my own—clearly, it was Julie's star and Julie's answer, in God's impeccable timing.

Julie and I marveled at how awesome God was, and even though I was the one who saw the star, we both knew it was for her. She and I sat in silence, looking out at the dark, expansive ocean, when another shooting star, taking the same path, shot across the sky.

This time we both saw it.

CHAPTER 15

After the earthquake came a fire, but the LORD was not in the fire. And after the fire came a gentle whisper.

1 Kings 19:12 NIV

One morning, I went to the bathroom a few minutes before it was time to get up. As I climbed back into bed, I was shocked to hear a small, still voice say: *Ben Geber five hundred.*

Ben Geber was the name of our worship leader, and one of the youth pastors at our church—it was Ben who had baptized our family in the ocean. It had been a privilege watching him mature and grow. Now he was a happily married father of two young children. I had heard that Ben and his family were moving to the mainland, but for various reasons, I hadn't talked with him for quite a while.

My first thought upon hearing *Ben Geber five hundred* was that we owed Ben five hundred dollars although I knew that wasn't the case. I tried to go back to sleep, but all I could think of was Ben and the audible voice.

During that day, I quickly surmised that God wanted Jack and I to *give* Ben five hundred dollars. At the time, that would have been a very generous gift, and I didn't know how to ask Jack about it. After all we'd been through, I knew it would be unsettling simply for me to tell him I'd heard a voice.

Because this was obviously a message from God, I knew that my timing had to be just right. For a full week I prayed about how to approach the subject, and I finally gathered up the nerve to say something on our way to church on Sunday.

I told Jack that I had a question, but that I wanted him to think carefully about it before he answered me.

Jack didn't say a word after hearing my story, and we walked into the sanctuary the same as we always did. During the message, our pastor talked about someone called Ben-Geber in the Bible.

Jack and I looked at each other, stunned by how God works. It was the first time either of us had heard there was a Ben Geber in the Bible.

After a few minutes, Jack looked at me with a slight smile, squeezed my hand tight, and nodded his head yes.

When church ended, Jack and I were so engrossed in our conversation that we didn't realize the sanctuary had emptied. Our pastor walked over and we told him what had happened.

We thought he'd be shocked, but he wasn't. I don't even think he was surprised—it was just one more God story to add to his collection.

That afternoon, Jack and I talked about how we could get the five hundred dollars to Ben. I didn't know exactly when Ben was moving, but I knew we needed to get the money to him as soon as possible.

Several days later I went shopping with Wyatt, and Ben

and one of his daughters walked in front of us as we were driving out of the parking lot.

I explained to Wyatt, "God has put it on our hearts to give Ben some money, probably to help with their moving expenses." I immediately turned the car around.

Ben and his daughter were sitting in a sandwich shop. Even though I felt like I was intruding upon his precious daddy-daughter time, I asked if we could talk with him for a minute. Ben welcomed us and asked us to have a seat.

We chatted for a few minutes, and then I told him what Jack and I had experienced concerning him. Like our pastor, Ben didn't seem overly surprised by anything I said.

I slid the five hundred-dollar check across the table, and Wyatt and I continued on our way.

On Ben's last Sunday in Hawaii, our pastor asked for a show of hands from those who had ever experienced a still, small voice in their life.

At first, no one put their hand up.

"Come on," Pastor Lee insisted. "Do you mean no one but me has ever heard a voice?"

Slowly, along with a few others, I raised my hand. Sitting there, I felt totally exposed, but surprisingly, I was okay with it.

That night was Ben's going-away party. It was a gorgeous Hawaiian night—the sky was filled with stars, and there was a slight breeze. One teenager after another got up to speak about how much Ben and his family meant to them. Many of them were crying as they said their "alohas."

As one person after another got up to talk about Ben, I debated whether or not to tell my story. I wanted to please the Lord, but didn't want to make Ben's night about me.

In the end, I decided to stay quiet. Every single person at the party knew that Ben's family would appreciate financial help—after all, moving to the mainland was expensive. And every single person knew that Ben was a man of God, with a godly family.

Most importantly, Ben already knew what my experience had reconfirmed for him—that God knew and loved him.

CHAPTER 16

Jesus said to her, "I am the resurrection and the life. The one who believes in me will live, even though they die; and whoever lives by believing in me will never die. Do you believe this?"

John 11:25-26 NIV

I had an older friend from my church named Carol who liked to speak her mind. She ruffled several feathers along the way, mine included… but I still loved her.

When I heard that Carol had fallen ill, it took several hours of thought and prayer to figure out how I could help her. Carol had only lived on the Big Island for a few years before she was diagnosed with cancer.

Carol and her husband, Dan, had been married for thirty-five years. They had four grown boys, two daughter-in-law's, and two precious grandchildren, all of whom lived in California.

Because she was bedridden, Carol knew that her purpose during this season of life was to pray fervently for her family.

Carol was a fierce prayer warrior, and I was privileged to pray with her on many occasions.

One of her sons, Hunter, was single—he was the one we prayed for the most. It was Hunter's desire—and Carol's desire for him—to meet a Christian woman, get married, settle down, and have children. I grew to adore Hunter, and Carol was not shy about showing me family pictures and telling me family stories.

Dan and Carol were a loving, committed couple, and I was blessed to help Dan with his sick wife for nearly a year. Because of my prayer time with Carol, when her boys came to Hawaii to say their final goodbyes, I felt as if I already knew them.

One day, Dan called to let me know that Carol was asking to see me. When I arrived, Hunter, who was a worship leader at his church, was playing the guitar and singing quietly to Carol. Seeing him singing to his mother was one of the sweetest moments I have ever witnessed.

Carol was extremely sick at this time, yet she was able to tell me that it was time to let her go. I had never told anyone that I was praying for Carol's miraculous healing, but somehow, she knew.

"Sarah, you have to let me go," she told me.

"Is that the way it works?" I asked, stunned.

Carol nodded her head. Several days later, she passed away peacefully. I never figured out what her comment meant, but I'm confident I will someday.

Through all of this, I grew to love the solid Christian woman that Carol was. Carol was also an artist, and a lover of words; consequently, our conversations were deep and interesting. I was intrigued by her passion to be creative in several different ways.

A few days after Carol died, I had a dream about her.

We were in a huge, clean, state-of-the-art studio. I was decorating the top of a small treasure box with a mosaic design. My box was fascinating—it was embellished by what looked like real jewels and small, blue-colored pieces of wood.

The blue wood was captivating, but not as captivating as the man standing next to me while I decorated the treasure box.

I felt so content to be by His side. It was Jesus!

The studio was suddenly empty except for Jesus and me. When He walked away, I chased after Him. To this day, I can still remember what that contentedness felt like—and it makes me long for the day when I will one day be with my Lord and Savior again.

Upon waking, I knew that God had given me that dream because of Carol. There was no interpretation needed. He wanted me to know that there was something incredible waiting for her artistic soul in heaven. Now, when I think of Carol, I picture her in the art studio with Jesus!

A couple of weeks after my dream, Dan told me there had been rainbow clouds in San Diego, where he had moved to be with his children shortly after Carol died.

There was even a picture of these rainbow clouds on the front page of one of the newspapers; apparently it was a rare atmospheric phenomenon.

Dan and I both saw this as a sign from God that as delighted as Carol was to be in heaven with Him, she wanted her family to know she hadn't forgotten them.

❧

Four years after Carol passed away, Hunter emailed me that he was coming to Hawaii with his new wife and son.

I was elated; I had heard he had gotten married and had a baby, but now I was going to get to meet them.

We met at a coffee shop late in the afternoon before they went to a luau on the beach. When I arrived, Hunter was holding 15-month-old Hank in the doorway of the coffee shop. Hank was one of the most beautiful children I had ever seen.

Hunter's equally beautiful—and very pregnant wife, Mary, came out of the coffee shop to introduce herself.

I was overcome with emotion. Here were two living, breathing answers to the prayers Carol and I had prayed. We sat down and Hunter told me their remarkable love story. As he talked, I could feel the abundance of blessings that had been poured out on this special young man.

Hunter was overwhelmed by God's love and generosity, and wanted me to share in his blessings. He also wanted me to know that I had met him during the saddest season of his life, but that we have a faithful Father in Heaven, who works everything out for the good of those who love Him.

It was a gift for me to have coffee with Hunter and his family. It was a gift to witness their love and listen to their hearts. I had no doubt that Carol would have been head over heels in love with Hank and Mary. For my part, I was a little taken aback by how strong my feelings were for little Hank. He drew me in like no other child had in the last twenty years, and I wonder if it was because I prayed for him with his grandmother.

When we said our alohas, I knew that Hunter and I would keep in touch.

At the same time that Hunter and his family were enjoying the luau on the beach, Jack and I were enjoying dinner on our lanai, where we were fortunate to enjoy amazing ocean and sunset views.

As I was telling Jack about my wonderful day, the biggest, brightest sun we had seen in years dropped from the clouds and sank into the ocean's horizon. It was then that I knew God was with us, rejoicing to have answered our prayers so spectacularly.

> *The whole earth is filled with awe at your wonders; where morning dawns, where evening fades, you call forth songs of joy.*
> *Psalm 65:8 NIV*

CHAPTER 17

Be alert and of sober mind. Your enemy the devil prowls around like a roaring lion looking for someone to devour.

1 Peter 5:8 NIV

Several years ago, I took Wyatt to Arizona for a week during the summer. I thought it would be a good idea to hang out with my brother and my nephew. Because of his drinking, John and his wife were separated at the time.

Night after night, I was plagued with terrible insomnia. There was a heaviness in John's house—which was eerily dark and dirty—that I couldn't explain.

On Sunday morning, I asked John and my nephew if they would like to attend a church that they loved, but which they hadn't visited in years.

To my delight, they both agreed to go. The pastor preached a sermon about his family being a guest in someone's home. The pastor's daughter couldn't sleep. The pastor had felt that the house was demon-oppressed when they entered—and when he asked the owner about it, the owner said that he felt it too.

The pastor decided to do something about it. He went through every room of the house and around the outside, praying and claiming it in Jesus' name.

It worked! Whatever was going on in that house disappeared, and the pastor's daughter was able to sleep at night.

Hearing his story, I wondered if that was what I was dealing with at John's house. I had been so focused on my own demonization, that demonic oppression in general wasn't even on my radar. The next day, when John's house was empty, I went through and claimed each room in Jesus' name. After cleaning John's home, I then made posters with scripture written on them and hung them up all over the house.

I started playing Christian music, and before I knew it, the house felt better. The oppression was gone—and it wasn't just an emotional feeling. It was a *physical* feeling. I could feel that the oppression had lifted, and from that point on I slept like a baby.

The mistake I made was not telling my brother what I did, and what I was experiencing. I didn't see my sister-in-law on that trip, but I did speak to her on the phone after she and my brother reconciled and she moved back home.

"You're going to think I'm crazy," she told me, "but there's something in the house. I can feel it."

"You're not crazy," I assured her. "I felt it too."

Thankfully, my sister-in-law was a strong Christian woman who not only cast the demons out of her house, but also investigated what was bringing them in in the first place. It turns out there was a lot of sin taking place in the house while my sister-in-law was gone. Those demons were just hanging out, waiting for a chance to wreak havoc.

CHAPTER 18

For God does speak—now one way, now another—though no one perceives it. In a dream, in a vision of the night, when deep sleep falls on people as they slumber in their beds, he may speak in their ears and terrify them with warnings, to turn from wrongdoing and keep them from pride, to preserve them from the pit, their lives from perishing by the sword.

Job 33:14-18 NIV

S ometimes, when everyone around me is fast asleep, myself included, God will give me a spiritual dream or a vision that stops me in my tracks. It only takes a split second for Him to get His message across.

The mystery to me is how He does it. How does God put a dream in our mind while we are sleeping?

There was a season in my life when I was involved in a situation with the Catholic church in our community, and I made an appointment with the priest. We talked the situation out, I thanked him for his time, and I left. However, the more I thought about our conversation, the more discouraged I got.

A few nights after my meeting with the priest, I had a dream.

"Grandma!... Wait... Grandma?" I said.

I was dreaming about the situation that brought me to the priest, and out of nowhere a picture of my grandmother popped into my mind. She had passed away years before, but in my dream, she was looking straight at me; the look on her face was angry, and I knew I needed to stop talking. I don't know what I was going to say, but I'm sure it was going to be something negative about the priest I had spoken with.

Even in a dream, I had the ability to stop gossiping—all because of one stern image of my grandmother.

My grandmother was a devout Catholic, so I'm certain it was she who insisted that I be baptized as an infant. She went into her room every single night at 8:00 and came back out half an hour later to wish us goodnight. During one visit, after several nights of watching my grandmother do this, I asked my dad what she was doing.

"Praying," he told me.

My grandfather had the super-sized personality, but it was my grandmother who never missed a birthday. She was quiet and thoughtful, and growing up I don't remember her ever getting angry.

In my dream, God was showing me that I was beginning to gossip and He stopped me in my tracks. That is how much He cares about dealing with gossip.

Jesus has shown me over the years how important it is not to talk about the church. The church is His bride. I know how I would feel if someone spoke negatively about

Jack, and that has helped keep me quiet. Pastors, priests, and church leaders are also God's anointed ones. Most people who truly desire to build God's Kingdom, or devote themselves to learning about God deserve to be respected. Of course, we can't keep quiet if we see abuse, but I have found if I'm dealing with something trivial, I'm better off holding my tongue. God's house needs to be a safe place for all.

God has also shown me that there are no perfect churches or people. It doesn't matter how wonderful someone is; if you spend enough time with them, they will probably disappoint you.

In his book *Devotions to a Deeper Life,* Oswald Chambers writes: "When will we learn that the best of men are but the best of men, and the best of women are but the best of women?"

There is only one Jesus Christ. The rest of us are mere, imperfect human beings. It's unrealistic to expect that we are going to live lifewith our brothers and sisters in Christ and *not* have disagreements. All we can do during those moments is our best. We can love them, learn from them, forgive them, and move on… together, and quickly! As believers, we are warriors for God's Kingdom, and we all have to keep that big picture in mind.

> *Those who guard their mouths and their tongues keep themselves from calamity.*
> *Proverbs 21:23 NIV*

Just when I think I have a handle on gossip, something happens that proves to me I don't. Gossip is a challenge for me—which is no surprise, as the Bible tells us that no one can tame their tongue.

One afternoon, I was chatting with my dear friends Lisa and Sue in our pool. Lisa casually said that because of a Bible Study she was in, she was going to do her best to stop gossiping. The problem was that she found herself gossiping more than she ever imagined she did.

"Everyone gossips at one time or another," I said—but as soon as I said it, I thought to myself that it was an odd thing to say. Neither Lisa nor Sue said anything.

That night, I had a short dream in which a huge black snake was slithering toward me. The snake was the only thing in my dream. Just as it opened its mouth—revealing impossibly large fangs—and lunged at me, I let out a gasp and woke up.

Feeling terrified and convicted, I knew that the Holy Spirit was cautioning me about gossip.

The next morning, I texted Lisa and Sue about my dream. Sue called right away.

"When you told us that everyone gossips at one time or another," she said, "my thought was that you are so much better than that."

I told Sue that God knows how petrified I have always been of snakes, and that he was using that vision to get His point across.

God hates gossip, and tells us that repeatedly throughout the Bible.

"Sarah, you're being too hard on yourself," Sue said. "How do you know that's what your dream was about?"

I just knew. The Holy Spirit was convicting me, and it didn't take much to get His point across.

Do not let any unwholesome talk come out of your mouths, but only what is helpful for

*building others up according to their needs,
that it may benefit those who listen.*
Ephesian 4:29 NIV

❧

In the late 1980s, my sister Anna and I were pregnant with our first-born children at the same time. It was exciting, envisioning the adorable little cousins playing together—but when Dustin, Anna's son, was a year and a half old, he died in a tragic accident.

Our entire family was devastated, and I personally felt as if I was never going to be happy again. While Jack and I believed in Jesus at the time, we didn't belong to a church or have any close Christian friends. The pain we felt was overwhelming. I tried reading the Bible, which helped a bit, but not in the way it would now. Because Anna and Dustin lived with my parents, their grief, in particular, was something I couldn't begin to comprehend.

Fortunately, my parents had a close Christian friend who spent time counseling them through the tragedy.

My mother started going to church, and several times sought God's peace and comfort by praying mid-week in the sanctuary by herself.

Meanwhile, I repeatedly asked God for a sign about Dustin. Instinctively, I knew that my sweet nephew was in heaven, but part of me needed some tangible proof.

After several years of praying about this, I simply stopped—God didn't seem to have anything to say to me about Dustin.

After Dustin's death, my family tried to express to Anna that she needed to change her highly destructive lifestyle, but my sister's life simply got darker.

A few years later, Anna had a little girl named Ava. My mother and stepfather helped raise Ava, just as they had Dustin. Ava quickly became the love of my parents' life. It wasn't an ideal situation, but Ava proved to be an incredible gift from God to all three of them, and she helped them all to heal.

More than two decades after Dustin's death, I had a vision with him in it. It was the first obvious gift that God had given me about Dustin. In my vision, Dustin, who seemed to be about eight years old, was lying on my parents' bed next to my mother; she was under the comforter, and he was on top of it. Dustin was fully dressed in jeans, a t-shirt, and sneakers. His hair was long, blond, and curly, just like Anna's hair when she was young. Dustin was grinning from ear to ear as he looked at me. He didn't speak, but he had the look of pure joy on his face because he was sitting next to his grandmother on her bed.

At first, I thought this was God's way of warning me that one of my parents was going to die. But in fact, He was telling me that everything was alright. This vision was a gift, an answer to my decades-long prayer.

What was most amazing to me was that God, in His perfect timing, decided to make me wait twenty-five years for a glimpse of Dustin—but the wait was worth it!

CHAPTER 19

How good and pleasant it is when God's
people live together in unity!
                                Psalm 133:1 NIV

When my precious father-in-law was passing away, Jack and I flew to Arizona, hoping to say goodbye, but fully aware that he had stopped speaking days before. Sadly, Dad passed away hours before we reached hospice, although his body was still in the room when we arrived.

When Jack embraced his mother, she slipped his father's turquoise inlaid watch onto Jack's wrist. It was such a sweet gesture for her to give it to him.

We followed Jack's mother home, and she went to the bedroom to gather other items of his father's that Jack might like. One thing she gave him was his father's turquoise inlaid wedding ring—it matched the watch perfectly.

Jack put it on and has kept it on since. Jack isn't overly

sentimental, and he doesn't talk much about his father being gone, but he wears that ring every day.

⋙⋘

One of my favorite people in the world is my friend Rory, who I've known for over twenty years. I love and admire her husband, Steve, as well.

The four of us get along famously; they live in California, but visit us in Hawaii several times each year. The time we spend together is delightful, except for the fact that Jack and I seem to gain a few pounds every time they visit. We eat differently when we're with them, which has become one of our running jokes.

One of our favorite things to do together is to go to the beach at sunset. Jack and Steve snorkel while Rory and I sit on the beach and chat about our lives.

One evening, we set up a couple of hours before sunset down on the bay. Steve and Jack went off to snorkel; I always found it endearing to watch the two of them enter the ocean together—but this time Jack came back, took off his father's ring, and handed it to me.

Rory and I were already in deep conversation by then, so I gave Jack a quick glance that said, "I've got it."

As I put the ring on my thumb, I realized how large it was, and wondered if it was loose on Jack's finger as well. As Rory and I were talking, an old neighbor of mine, Nancy, walked by. I jumped up to greet her and received such a warm, tight hug that I was a little taken aback. When I pulled away to look at her, I was surprised by her transformation from the last time I'd seen her; God had obviously been doing a mighty work in her and her family's life.

We chatted for ten minutes before Steve and Jack

returned from their snorkeling. Jack couldn't believe Nancy's countenance either- she was positively glowing.

As the sun started to set, we said our goodbyes. Steve and Jack were famished, and decided that Chinese food sounded good. We had an enjoyable dinner, said good night and headed home. The entire time, Jack and I continued to marvel at how well our old neighbor seemed to be doing.

When we got back home, Jack said, "Sarah, where'd you put my dad's ring?"

My eyes grew wide as saucers.

My mind went blank.

Twirling the ring on my finger, thinking how big it was, was the last time I remembered thinking about it. From that moment on, I had no memory of his dad's ring. NONE. I remembered jumping up to hug Nancy, and decided that's when and where it must have fallen off.

Jack and I grabbed our cellphones and headed back to the beach. Jack kept telling me, "It's not your fault; I shouldn't have worn it to the beach."

I had no reply. I knew it was my fault. How could I have been so reckless with my father-in-law's wedding ring? We both dreaded telling Jack's mom what happened; it would break her heart.

We parked exactly where we had before, turned our flashlights on, and began searching. We thought that perhaps it was in the beach chair, and had fallen out when we put it in the back of the truck. We searched the sidewalk and grass area all the way back to the beach, but had no luck. The beach was dimly lit from a nearby restaurant.

A light rain began to fall. Slowly, Jack and I searched the path we thought we had taken to "our spot." First, we searched the top of the sand, and then started shuffling row by row with our feet.

Sadly, the ring was nowhere to be found.

I remembered hearing about someone losing a ring and hiring a man with a metal detector to find it. I suggested that Jack check the nearby resorts to see if anyone had turned in a ring—and, if not, to ask if they knew anyone with a metal detector. Jack ran off to ask around.

Meanwhile, I saw a young woman on the beach who was obviously upset. As we had been searching for the ring, she had been talking on her cellphone and crying. When Jack left, she walked over and asked if she could help us look for the ring.

She said it would be good for her. I asked if she was okay; she told me she was going through some "boy drama."

Another man walked up, asked what we were looking for, and started hunting with us. Jack came back talking on his phone; he was setting up an appointment with a man who had a metal detector. He said he would meet us the next morning.

The four of us said goodbye and God bless, and we headed home. Praying before we went to sleep that night, Jack and I both agreed it was hard to be content in this situation, but Jesus was giving us the strength to do just that.

The next morning Lew, the man with the metal detector, called and asked where he should begin looking. I threw on a hat and a cover-up and drove to meet him. There was still a light tropical rain falling all the way from my house to the beach.

I parked in the same spot as the night before. As I looked down, searching for the ring in the daylight, I saw a beautiful feather lying on the street. It made me feel a bit hopeful about finding the ring, but part of me was convinced we weren't going to. I had been praying off and on since I lost the ring, and finally concluded that God's will be done.

What interested me more than anything was what God had in store for us because of this.

Because it was sprinkling, the beach was empty except for Lew. I pointed him in the right direction, sat under a palm tree, and began to pray. While I was praying, God put it on my heart to ask my girlfriends for prayer. That hadn't even occurred to me.

I didn't want them to know how irresponsible I had been with my beloved father-in-law's wedding ring. The longer that Lew searched, the more I argued with myself.

Finally, I asked myself what the most important outcome here was. Was I so prideful that I wasn't willing to reach out and ask my sisters in Christ to pray?

I took a picture of Lew out on what seemed like an enormous beach with endless grains of sand, and sent it to the girls with a prayer request. Several of them replied immediately, and a rainbow formed behind Lew.

I took another picture, and began to feel more hopeful. Within a minute of sending the request, Lew bent down, picked up the ring, and walked over to me with a huge smile on his face.

I couldn't believe it! I gave Lew a big hug.

Where had my faith been? Of course, Lew found the ring; he had made it look easy. I took a picture of Lew smiling, holding up my father-in-law's ring. There was still a rainbow behind him.

I sent the picture to the girls with the caption, "He found it!!"

The girls couldn't believe how quickly Lew had found the ring. That's when I realized that asking the girls to join me in prayer had made all the difference.

As I was driving home, Jack called, but I didn't answer. Selfishly, I decided he could wait another ten minutes before finding out. I wanted to see the look on his face when he saw the ring.

Jack was still getting ready for work when I walked into the bedroom holding the ring up for him to see. With tears in his eyes, he grabbed me and gave me the biggest hug ever.

"I can't believe it," he said.

He put the ring on, and we were both surprised to see how shiny the sand had polished it. What a great start to the day; now we never had to explain to my mother-in-law that I had lost her husband's ring.

That day, I started thinking about my prayer warrior friends and feeling grateful for my church; otherwise, I'm sure I never would have met them.

I know there are a lot of strong believers in the world who don't go to church for one reason or another. There are so many real and potential conflicts of belief and interests, so many different personalities. We are all imperfect people living in a fallen world.

For me, however, countless blessings have come from belonging to a church.

I love meeting with other believers and fellowshipping with them. I love worshipping the Lord with my church family. I love serving at my church and teaching Sunday school to the little ones. And I love tithing. I love giving back to God what is His in the first place.

I love the Father, Son, and Holy Spirit with all my heart. I love to read my Bible, because it's God's written word to us, and I love the unity of the church. Before Jesus was arrested in the garden of Gethsemane, He prayed for unity.

"My prayer is not for them alone. I pray also
for those who will believe in me through

their message, that all of them may be one,
Father, just as you are in me and I am in
you. May they also be in us so that the world
may believe that you have sent me. I have
given them the glory that you gave me, that
they may be one as we are one— I in them
and you in me— so that they may be brought
to complete unity. Then the world will know
that you sent me and have loved them even
as you have loved me.

John 17:20-23 NIV

One morning after some friends and I had enjoyed our coffee and prayer time together, we started talking about how grateful we were that only Jesus has the ability to save people. However, as grateful as we were to be saved, and to serve as Jesus' hands and feet, having the responsibility of sharing the gospel can feel overwhelming- and even impossible- at times.

Our conversation morphed into one of sowing seeds that would grow into shade trees that we could sit under with our friends in times of trouble. Feeling content, surrounded by women I truly considered my sisters in Christ, I had that warm and fuzzy feeling knowing that this was the life God had created for me.

Had Jesus not SAVED me, and given me the desire to change, none of that would have happened.

A few days after our meeting, I flew to Arizona to visit family. On Sunday morning, I decided to go to the church where Jack and I had first accepted Jesus so many years ago.

As I walked into the church, there was a huge tree on the stage in a wooden crate. It was so big, I'm sure they had to use a forklift to bring it in.

That pastor started talking about planting seeds that grow into shade trees. He was talking about the church, and how, over the years, that is what it had become to the community—a place of safety and shelter.

He was talking about what my girlfriends back home and I had been talking about, except on a much larger scale.

Because I depend on God continually, my entire perspective has changed over the years. God has given me a heavenly perspective on life. He is constantly helping me to see situations from His perspective.

I often see what I believe are miracles happening, while others see only natural occurrences and coincidences instead of divine appointments, or instead of the Holy Spirit working in or around us. That morning I sat in the church stunned, reveling in the fact that God was with me, and that He was at work letting me know that I was His.

After the service was over, as I walked out the door, the ushers handed each person a small bag of seeds. The pastor had suggested that we all work at becoming shade trees for those around us in their time of need.

I smiled, thankful to God for His unity.

CHAPTER 20

"Haven't you read," he replied, "that at the beginning the Creator 'made them male and female,' and said, 'For this reason a man will leave his father and mother and be united to his wife, and the two will become one flesh'? So they are no longer two, but one flesh. Therefore what God has joined together, let no one separate."

Matthew 19:4-6 NIV

It was God who got Jack and I through the darkest period of our marriage. After being demonically invaded, finding out about Jack's infidelity, and then dealing with the lingering effects of PTSD from both, it was God who was constantly reminding us of our love for one another. Ours was a long and difficult struggle, but God kept us together. He loves us and knows what motivates us as individuals; more importantly, He knows what motivates us to stay together.

Jack and I believed in God's promises in the Bible, and had faith that He would restore what we had thought was broken beyond repair. My faith is in God, and I will keep moving forward and believing that God is in charge of my life and my marriage. He knows what is best for us and so far, whatever He's doing is working.

Jack and I just do our best to keep doing the next right thing.

I trust that God's big picture is bigger than ours ever could be. God and I have a history together, and He has always proven himself to be my protector. I trust Him not only with my life, but with my family's life.

God created all of us, and whatever happens to us, I have to remember that His love is so much greater than mine could or ever will be. God is love. The God that governs my life is love! How incredible is that?

What kind of world would it be if we looked at our spouse the way God looks at them? Can you imagine looking at another human being through God's eyes? Can you imagine seeing their entire life from start to finish, and completely understanding why they said or did something?

Realistically, if two people love the Lord and make Him their priority in life, they can make it through almost anything. It won't necessarily be easy—staying with Jack was one of the most difficult decisions I have ever made in my life. But I knew that we were both sinful human beings slowly being transformed and sanctified by the supernatural work of the Holy Spirit.

As odd as it may sound, I will always be thankful that I did not find out about Jack's infidelity until we had been married almost a quarter of a century. Because of that, we had plenty of time to create some incredible memories. I also thank God in advance for the incredible memories we are going to make together in the future... not only as a couple, but as a family.

Jack and I are empty nesters now, and try to be humble and gentle with one another. We're not perfect, but we're doing our best to love one another and live a healthy lifestyle together. Keeping up with "Super Jock" has never been easy, but I'm doing a decent job.

We pray together often, and respect one another's thoughtful decisions more. We avoid situations that might cause another "storm" in our lives. God has taught us how important our relationship is, and we make it a priority. Communication and compromise are more a part of our lives than they ever were.

Jack and I like the life God is helping us to create together, which is something I never thought I would say in the midst of our trials. Jack is my person. When I chose to marry him, I chose a story, a story that we were going to write for the rest of our lives.

I had a choice to make after all of the trauma and betrayal. I could choose to live my life as a victim of my circumstances in fear and bitterness, or I could transform my pain, learn from it, and become a blessing to others for the glory of God.

Because I love Jesus so much, I chose the second option.

❧

One night, shortly after returning from a wonderful trip to the mainland, I could hear Jack moving around, but he wasn't saying anything. He was making an odd sound.

I turned on the light and Jack was lying on the bed, staring at the ceiling. He was making a gurgling sound. Terrified, I jumped out of bed. Jack was having an asthma attack and had misplaced his inhaler. I made a mad dash looking for it; just as I was ready to call 9-1-1, I found his inhaler under the bed.

Jack got his breathing under control and went back to sleep; meanwhile, I lay there shaken to my core.

"What just happened?" I thought. What would have happened if I weren't here? How am I ever going to go to the mainland by myself again? Really, God, after all these years we finally get our marriage to a place I thought we'd never see again, and Jack almost dies?

I didn't know what to think.

The next morning, Jack and I agreed that he needed a backup inhaler, and we needed to double-check that it was next to him every night. The most eye-opening part of the whole incident was that I had no idea how much Jack depended on his inhaler to survive.

All day long I thought about how much I loved Jack, how much we had been through, and how broken we both were—and yet that somehow, God had helped us to overcome it. Our marriage and family had not only survived incredible odds, but were thriving—and just like that, Jack could have been gone. I could be a widow today, except for the grace and mercy of our faithful God.

Jack must have been thinking the same thing, because that night he woke me up again, this time by saying my name in his sleep. He didn't just say my name, he *sang* it. I had never heard anything like it before, and quickly realized it was from God.

As I lay in bed praying, God put it on my heart that He wanted to show me Jack's heart, and He did.

> Our mouths were filled with laughter, our tongues with songs of joy. Then it was said among the nations, "The LORD has done great things for them."
>
> Psalm 126:2 NIV

CHAPTER 21

*Put on the full armor of God, so that you can
take your stand against the devil's schemes.*
Ephesians 6:11 NIV

O ne day my friend Avery asked me if I would help
her throw a church fundraiser. Avery, the mother
of a beautiful three month old baby girl, was
feeling understandably overwhelmed by all of her duties.

Fundraisers aren't my favorite thing, but I enjoy
helping people, so I said yes. This was a pretty simple lunch
fundraiser, and I thought I had everything under control
until the night before. I started Googling some questions I
had concerning the food preparation for the fundraiser, and
before I knew it, I couldn't sleep!

I tossed and turned all night long, finally rolling out of
bed at 6 am. I was tired, but excited, as I headed out of the
house feeling prepared for the big day. On the way to church
I listened to worship music, all the while praying that the
fundraiser would go smoothly.

By the time I got to church, I felt as though I were

literally radiating Christ's light as I walked onto the property. It didn't take long, however, to be hit by the realities of the day.

Everywhere I went I was confronted with some crisis: chaotic directions, unrealistic needs, harsh or hurtful words, and my own observations of things that were off. I got to the point where I was almost afraid to engage in conversation. I was, however, determined to keep shining Jesus' light. This fundraiser was for Jesus, and I was doing my best to represent Him.

With her infant safely wrapped to her, Avery was oblivious to my dismay, and seemed delighted that the fundraiser was such a big success. I, on the other hand, was shell-shocked. After the event was over, several people helped Jack and I clean and pack up, and then we were off.

When we got home, friends started texting me how great the fundraiser was, while I was thinking how glad I was that it was over. Avery texted me saying that if we threw the fundraiser again next year we should do it exactly the same way. She thought it was perfect. I had never known her to lie, but assumed that in this case she was exaggerating to protect my feelings. I wanted to tell her that next year I'd be more than happy to write a check matching whatever we made this year, just to get out of actually having to participate again!

While I was recuperating, the next day I wrote down a list of everything I had endured the day before. It didn't take long for me to realize that I was in the midst of a spiritual battle. The devil hates the church, and everything we try to accomplish in Jesus' name.

From the minute I got out of the car at church until I was getting in my car to leave, I was under attack. Fortunately, I kept my mouth closed, and fortunately I was the one people were directing their frustrations at- not Avery, the sweet new mom. Avery wasn't a new Christian, but she was young.

Not only does the devil prowl around looking to kill, steal, and destroy, we have the inadvertent ability to do the same with our words. Through faith, maturity, and experience, most of us know that whatever trials we are going through are temporary; but a careless word to a new or young Christian can send them running for the hills, never to return.

It is easy to get "church hurt." It takes strength in the Lord to bounce back from that, but it's crucial. We are human beings—and because no one except God is perfect, I am learning to be resilient and forgiving in situations that before Christ would have seemed impossible.

After writing out my list of experiences at the fundraiser, I realized that sometimes praying and worshipping the Lord is not enough. I needed my armor on. I needed to remember that something like the fundraiser was going to produce great results for God's kingdom, and that Satan hates that.

We were all warriors going into battle, and we needed protection. We needed to be reminded of the battle, and that our enemy was going to try and take us down. We needed to be proactive to prevent this.

We usually prayed as a group before our events, but because I arrived at a different time, I didn't.

I got out my Bible and read Ephesians 6:10-20 NIV. God covered me in His peace which surpasses all understanding, and I was restored:

> Finally, be strong in the Lord and in his mighty power. Put on the full armor of God, so that you can take your stand against

the devil's schemes. For our struggle is not against flesh and blood, but against the rulers, against the authorities, against the powers of this dark world and against the spiritual forces of evil in the heavenly realms. Therefore put on the full armor of God, so that when the day of evil comes, you may be able to stand your ground, and after you have done everything, to stand. Stand firm then, with the belt of truth buckled around your waist, with the breastplate of righteousness in place, and with your feet fitted with the readiness that comes from the gospel of peace. In addition to all this, take up the shield of faith, with which you can extinguish all the flaming arrows of the evil one. Take the helmet of salvation and the sword of the Spirit, which is the word of God. And pray in the Spirit on all occasions with all kinds of prayers and requests. With this in mind, be alert and always keep on praying for all the Lord's people. Pray also for me, that whenever I speak, words may be given me so that I will fearlessly make known the mystery of the gospel, for which I am an ambassador in chains. Pray that I may declare it fearlessly, as I should.

The next day I walked the beach with my friends Lisa and Sue. I told them about my experience at the fundraiser.

When I told them what I had decided about making sure I had my armor on from now on, they agreed with me.

That evening, Avery called and I told her everything I had gone through. She listened patiently, and afterwards she said, "I'm so sorry you went through all of that, but I have to tell you, I was stress-free. Usually my family feels the brunt of it all, but not with this fundraiser."

"Then it was all worth it," I told her, knowing that the next time, I would definitely have my armor on.

CHAPTER 22

*For I know the plans I have for you,"
declares the LORD, "plans to prosper you
and not harm you, plans to give you hope
and a future.*

Jeremiah 29:11 NIV

Almost two years after they were married by the Justice of the Peace in New York City, Ryan, our oldest son, and his bride, Juliana, planned a marriage celebration in Brazil. We were finally going to celebrate Ryan and Juliana's special love story with them, their dearest friends, and Juliana's family. The event was something we had all been looking forward to with great anticipation.

On our way to the celebration, we scheduled a stop in Arizona to see our family. My brother and sister-in-law were once again separated. After hearing a pastor's sermon on addictions being a form of demonic control and how common it was, God put it on my heart that John's alcoholism was really demonization and I needed to cast the demon out.

As serious as this was, I did not want to go into it alone and brought the subject up with Lisa and Sue. They were very familiar with John's story, as we had discussed it many times over the years. They agreed to pray for John in Hawaii, at the same time I was casting the demon out in Arizona. At the time, I had no idea where I would do it, but I was determined. We also discussed the fact that because he had been on a binge, he would be in rough shape. I might not want to leave him to go to Brazil for the celebration. I assured them I would not miss it. That would break Ryan's heart.

I called John and made plans to go to church and lunch the Sunday after we arrived. After I hung up the phone, God put it on my heart that church was where I would pray for John's demons to be cast out. I speak from experience when I say, church is a hospital for the broken because that is where a lot of my own healing has come from. I was nervous, but excited. The pieces were coming together.

Sunday morning Jack and I picked John up. As glad as I was to see him, it made me sad to see the shape he was in. He was shaky and could hardly walk. His color was off and his speech was slow. He had stopped drinking the day before and was having withdrawals. Suddenly, I was afraid for him. Jack and I debated whether we should take him into church or not, but decided it was the right thing to do.

We found a seat in the back. The worship band led us in the first song. Jack and I stood up with the rest of the church, but John was too weak to stand. With tears in my eyes, I texted Lisa and Sue to ask them for prayer and put my hand on John's back. In faith, while praising and worshipping the Lord, in Jesus' name, I demanded the demons leave John's body.

To my surprise, John was able to make it through the entire service. We thought it odd, however, that he didn't have an appetite at lunch. We dropped him off and went to see my parents. They needed to know he wasn't doing well.

The next day, we headed to Brazil.

The celebration was spectacular- beyond our wildest dreams and something none of us will ever forget. It was such a joyous occasion, and more than we could ever have imagined. Both Ryan and Juliana said it was the best day of their lives!

One of the highlights of the celebration, for me, was Juliana's cousin, Pablo, the Christian pastor who spoke at the celebration. His message was so beautiful and Holy Spirit filled. He loved Jesus the way we loved Jesus! Feeling blessed beyond measure, the entire day left us feeling overwhelmed by God's incredible love and unity.

After the celebration, Ryan and Juliana spent the rest of the trip with our family. We traveled a bit and got to see and experience some of the country and culture. On top of everything else, Ryan and Wyatt were able to surf! A great time was had by all!

Just as we were preparing to leave Brazil and head back to the United States, I received a call from my mother. She had been trying to get a hold of John with no luck, so she and my sister drove to his house. They found John lying on the floor..... unresponsive. Only God knows how long he was in that condition. My mother told me that John was in the hospital and they did not know if he was going to live or not.

It had finally happened. That was the phone call I had been dreading my entire adult life.

It took us a day to get to Arizona. John was awake when we arrived at the hospital, but he was extremely weak. His skin was the color of mustard and nothing he said made sense. My sister-in-law overheard a nurse say she had never seen anyone survive who was in that condition. The doctor said John was in kidney and liver failure, and then he told us that John only had three to six months to live. They put John on palliative care with the hope that it would relieve his suffering.

I had no idea what to pray for, so I prayed for God's will to be done. God knew all the details and what the outcome was going to be. All Jack and I could do was be there for John and our family.

His friends came to say their good-byes.

Our extended family did the same.

Our dad, whom both John and I had had a rocky relationship with our entire adult lives, called often. A widower in his 80's, and in poor health himself, he was unable to travel to say goodbye.

John was in the hospital for three weeks, after that, he went into a rehabilitation center. He still had no strength and basically needed to learn how to walk again. Against all odds, he seemed to be improving. None of us believed he was going to die anytime soon. The problem was, we did not know how he was going to live either. He was still not himself, and continued to talk nonsense.

The rehabilitation center got John up and walking again, but because he couldn't live by himself anymore, John's wife, Laurie, generously invited him to move in with her. There wasn't a lot Jack or I could do to help, so we went home.

While we were in Hawaii, John's doctor gave him his diagnosis.

We thought John's cirrhosis of the liver along with kidney and heart failure were the main concerns, until the doctors diagnosed John with Alcoholic Dementia.

We had never heard of Alcoholic Dementia— but it made sense.

We were thankful John was alive, but confused about how he was going to live that life.

There was no getting a job. No driving. No even going out for a walk by himself. For the most part, he had lost his short term memory skills. He was only 58 years old. My sister-in-law was doing a remarkable job of keeping John safe and content, but at some point she was going to need help.

That's when Jack and I seriously started talking about moving back to Arizona full time. At that point we had lived in Hawaii for almost 20 years. Ryan and Addy had long moved away and our youngest, Wyatt, was a senior in college on the mainland. As much as he loved island living, he didn't see himself moving back to Hawaii for a while... if ever.

Even though I was going to miss my wonderful friends, church, community and life in Hawaii—for me—it was time to go. After more conversation and prayer, Jack finally agreed, for now, our time in Hawaii had come to an end.

It was a quick move. We packed the belongings we wanted to keep into a moving container, and shipped it to Arizona. The hardest part, by far, was saying 'aloha' to our dear friends and church family. What gave me great comfort was knowing that because we are eternal beings, the believers we know and love today, we will know and love for eternity!

Just a couple of days before we were to leave Hawaii, I had to drive into town to run some errands. Driving south into town, a bright white flash in the sky caught my eye. As I looked up, I noticed a bunch of black birds sitting on the telephone lines. In the middle of the birds was a lone white bird. It was the bright white birds glow that had caught my eye!

As I drove, I prayed asking God for the millionth time, "who was I to Him?" I know who the Bible says I am, but how was I ever going to really understand why the Creator of the universe would care to know me. Immediately, God put it on my heart that this is who I and countless others are to Him: I have been washed clean by the blood of the Lamb. Righteous to the Father because I love and obey His Son. Knowing from now on that I would always stand out to God alone or in a crowd- not because of anything else but that I believed. My body is a temple for the Holy Spirit. I am a daughter of the Most High and I want to shine as brightly as that little white bird for all the world to see because Jesus is mine and I am His. In an instant, I finally got it! It all made sense, and I was set free!

> *But if we walk in the light, as he is in the light, we have fellowship with one another, and the blood of Jesus, his Son, purifies us from all sin.*
>
> *1 John 1:7 NIV*

Scottsdale, Arizona

Before we knew it, we were back in Scottsdale, living the Arizona life.

It's been an amazing thing to watch my brother and his wife reconcile. It has not been easy, but their family is together and John is not drinking. Only God could have done that.

We're much closer to our family and children now and get to see everyone more often. That makes us happy.

We also feel blessed to have found a Spirit filled church that we love.

Before I left Hawaii, Lisa and Sue generously offered to start our own little Bible Study and we group chat most Thursday mornings. That has been pure joy and one of the highlights of my week!

I look forward to PTSD being a thing of the past for me. I know that in Jesus all things are possible. It's my understanding that the sooner someone receives professional help after a terrifying event, the better their prognosis. I did receive help right away after I was demon indwelt, it just wasn't the spiritual kind of help I required. Because this continues to be an issue in my life, as soon as we moved to Arizona, I found a Christian Counselor, who specializes in PTSD. What I have learned is there is so much help available for PTSD that no one needs to suffer with this alone. My counselor is helping me to live in the here and now and feel safe. I'm making progress and I thank God for her.

For a long time now, both Jack and I have had a desire to travel the United States. We long to see more of God's beautiful creation and what's going on in America. Because Jack is working from home now, we don't need to live a conventional lifestyle. After much discussion, God led us to buying a motorhome… something I never thought we would own, but I was wrong. So far Jack and I love it!

I am so grateful for this adventure God has given us and continues to take us on. The good, the great, the bad, and the ugly… all of it, because this is my journey to Him.

Yes, I came to salvation much differently than most people do, but because of Jesus, I am SAVED and will be eternally grateful. I am going to heaven, and I am going to be with my Lord and Savior for eternity.

His ways are so much more than ours ever could be… if we would only listen.

❧

I wrote this book because my story isn't just about being temporarily controlled by a demon, but about being restored by Jesus. It isn't just a story of Jesus' supernatural abilities, but of a repentant heart that followed. Knowing God is a lifelong process, and it is my hope that no one will read this book and put it on their bookshelf. It is my hope that you will pass it on to someone you care about.

The world is watching; our life's story is written on our friends and family's hearts. The obstacles we face today can help others with what they will face tomorrow. Over the years, God has taught me to point others who are suffering in His direction because He is where our hope comes from.

It is the nature of our lives here on earth to have challenges. At some point, we have to make a transition and look at our challenges with absolute trust that everything God is doing is going to work out for His glory.

Maybe it's time that we change the way we look at our trials and tribulations and consider them gifts--gifts of life lessons and blessings. Gifts that we can pass on to our loved ones so they don't make the same mistakes. One of the most important gifts we can give to those we care about is to be completely truthful and vulnerable because we love them; because we want to spare them unnecessary heartache and wasted precious time.

Each of us was given an allotted amount of time to seek God, and only God knows when we are going to die. Jesus has told us over and over in the Bible that He wants us in heaven with Him. Hell simply cannot be an option for us or our loved ones! Do we really believe our Heavenly Father would crush, bruise and kill His only begotten Son, but let us slide?

This book is an act of love from me to you because of Jesus. I am in love with my Lord and Savior and I will live the rest of my life thanking Him. My hope is that you, too, will feel God's redeeming love and be grateful for your life right where God has you now-- the lessons He has given you and the lessons He has in store for you. God loves you so much!

Because I am so grateful to God for the countless ways He has taken care of me, I would like to continue to give back to Him. The majority of the proceeds of this book will go toward helping children at risk of not hearing the word of God, come to know and love Christ. It is my hope that as they grow, they will have a deep desire to share the Gospel and help others along the way.

It is time for change! Let's be world changers!

That starts by becoming Jesus followers.

It's my prayer that you will walk away understanding that the spiritual realm is real. Satan is real. Intimacy with God creates a life of miracles; and the Father, the Son, and the Holy Spirit are the most important persons in our life.

Heaven is real. I hope to see you there one day.

EPILOGUE

*For God so loved the world that he gave his
one and only Son, that whoever believes in
him shall not perish but have eternal life.*

John 3:16 NIV

It is my sincere hope that this book has touched you the way God has intended it to. It is my prayer that you would desire the same relationship that I and countless others experience with Jesus Christ, our Lord and Savior. Below is a prayer to get you started. It is a prayer asking Jesus for His forgiveness, to come into your life, to be your foundation and the rock on which you stand.

> *Dear Lord,*
>
> *Thank you for loving me, and thank you for listening to me. Only You know how weak I am. Only You know the hurt and resentment I've faced. Only You know the things that have been done to me, and only You know what I have done to others. Right now, Lord Jesus, I come to You and ask for Your forgiveness. I am trusting Your death*

on the cross to be the only payment for my sins. I ask for Your cleansing, and I ask You to send your Holy Spirit to take over my life. From this moment on, I am Yours, Jesus, and You are mine.

In Your Holy and Precious name Jesus I pray,

Amen

Father, for those who have prayed this prayer, I pray You would allow the anointing of Your Holy Spirit to come into their lives here and now.

Amen, and may God bless you always.